Table of Contents

I would like to dedicate this to all the countless people who have prayed for me, especially those called by the Lord to pray for me in the challenging seasons that came after I prayed, asking the Lord to "crush me like an olive pit to get the good oil out." I would not be who I am today without those prayers as well as the direct intervention of the Lord when I was so clearly off track in my life. Thank you to those who have extended me grace and to those who have encouraged me as I tried my best to encourage others to step into their own new life in Christ. A sincere "Thank You" to all who have held me accountable and consistently pointed me back to Jesus - May you be Blessed beyond measure!

Introduction

Raising Up Leaders

I am deeply honored that you are reading my book. I hope that you find what it is that you are in need of within these pages. I hope that my testimony blesses you and encourages you to go after your own next level of freedom in Christ and that some of the tools which the Lord shared with me end up being effective for you as well. You are born to be a leader and I believe with all my heart that Jesus is extremely excited to see how you pursue what it is that He puts in front of you.

One of my favorite Parables is the one about the Kingdom of Heaven being like a field (Matthew 13:44) in which a man finds a treasure that is so valuable to him that he hides it and then he goes and sells everything he has of worth that he may by that entire field! Father God looked down and He saw us stuck in the world and He gave His only begotten Son (John 3:16) that we might be set free from whatever had us bound and stuck. Because of Jesus Christ of Nazareth and what He accomplished on the Cross, we are able to enter into the relationship of a lifetime and become a treasure within the Kingdom of God. We are able to finally become the person that He made us to be!

The challenge is that we do not yet see things as He does. We don't yet think as He does. *"For no eye has* seen, nor ear heard, nor the heart of man imagined what it is that He is preparing for those who love Him." (1 Corinthians 2:9) We just aren't there yet, but God is always inviting us to come ever closer - to take a look at what's inside His heart for us. I don't know about you, but I know that I have a pretty creative imagination and I still know that what He is doing is vastly bigger than I could even begin to imagine. That is simply amazing!

I also believe that Father God wants us to dream with Him. He wants us to partner with Him in order to bring His kingdom to Earth as it is in Heaven (Matthew 6:10). He doesn't just want us to have the dreams that He puts in our minds, He wants us to take those things to an even higher level. One way that we can do this is to realize that there is still "empty ground" and we can plant Kingdom seeds within those fields and then He can bring them to life, in the Name of Jesus.

I believe that each one of us also has treasure (2 Corinthians 4:7) deep within us that simply needs to be breathed upon in order for it to come to life. Words of Encouragement can be given to others that will cause them to blossom and bloom and develop into who it is that God has always known they would be. When we share Hope with the hopeless, it gives them something to hold onto and it can be enough to turn their circumstances around in a way that is barely even recognizable. All because Hope walked in to the situation and it completely shifted! We are all called to encourage one another. The greatest charge that Jesus gave to the

Body of Christ is to edify one another (1 Thessalonians 5:11). We are to build others up. To train them and equip them so that they can come into alignment with who it is that Father God is calling them to be for a Time such as This. Yes, there are different seasons of development within our Christian walk and within these seasons sometimes we are at a moment of gathering information into our hearts so that it can become a part of our Spirit man and then we can leap forward acting upon it. Other times, we are already running in all out in pursuit of Jesus. Sometimes we find ourselves being taught and other times we are the Teacher. In all of this, Jesus is the constant. He's the one we look to in order to discover who it is that He wants us to be for each given person we encounter on each given day.

On the day that Jesus was baptized by John the Baptist, the heavens parted and Father God announced from Heaven: "this is my Son in whom I am well pleased." (Matthew Chapter 3) With that He announced Jesus' full identity: A son who was well Loved. Once Jesus began training His disciples, He very clearly and emphatically told them *"I only do what I see the Father doing. I only say what the Father says!"* (John 5:19) Jesus was continuously looking to His Father to learn what it was that His Father wanted to bring forth in each and every situation. Upon the Mount Transfiguration, the heavens once again opened and Father God Himself announced once again: *"this is my son in whom I am well pleased!"* He then added: *"Hear Him!"* (Matthew Chapter 17) I believe that at this particular moment, Father God was actually passing the baton of Leadership directly to Jesus. I believe that it is vital for us to actually look to Jesus in each and every situation because when we see Jesus, we see the Father (John 14:9) and then we will know exactly what it is that He wants brought forth for His kingdom on Earth as it is in Heaven.

We need to pray unceasingly (1 Thessalonians 5:16) for one another that we would continue to hear the Lord clearly and that we would wait on His perfect timing as we pursue His very best for our own lives and for the lives of others. God is the King of breakthrough and because we see the tapestry from the bottom and not from God's perspective yet, we need to realize that we have a tendency to categorize people by looking at a snapshot in time. In reality, each person is continuously evolving and none of us truly knows what another person's final position or what their Divine Purpose is. What we do know, but maybe sometimes forget, is that neither the Kingdom nor the Bride will be complete or whole until every single one of us is in our unique and proper position, walking in the fullness of what Jesus accomplished for us upon the Cross. For this reason, we need to continually listen to the Holy Spirit and hear how the Lord wants to activate and edify others.

The Bible tells me that *"as we measure so shall we meet"* (Matthew 7:2) and since I know that I want to be encouraged myself when I meet the Lord face to face, I choose to be about my Father's business, encouraging others each and every day. I choose to pray unceasingly as I walk in love, demonstrating the power of His love to each and every one I meet. I don't want to meet the Lord face-to-face and learn that I missed any opportunities to advance His Kingdom.

Christian Tension - Being Not of this World

As Christians who are no longer of this world but still have to live within the world (John 15:19), we find ourselves suspended between the two ends of the pendulum. We are somewhere between aiming for full Kingdom consciousness with regards to how would Father God, Jesus, and the Holy Spirit have us live out each moment and the pressure created by our culture as it tells us what it is we need in order to succeed within the world. We oftentimes find ourselves stuck in the middle of the tension between the demands of our culture and the demands of Christianity when we truly surrender Lordship of our lives to Jesus Christ, our King.

Years ago, there was a slogan that became popular that asked "What would Jesus do? Or WWJD" I believe that was satan trying to make a mockery of the demands placed upon followers of Jesus. He is always trying to undermine what it is that God offers us through Jesus Christ and the Holy Spirit. The reality of the matter is that we lose absolutely nothing by becoming a Believer in Jesus Christ and making Him the Lord Of Our Lives, rather, we gain life and life more abundant (John 10:10) while on Earth along with eternal life once our assignment here is completed.

This book is meant to be a lesson in Hope; by sharing my Testimony of how the Lord was always faithful despite my many stumblings, I believe you too will be encouraged. In sharing my Testimony along with some of the Spiritual tools that the Holy Spirit equipped me with in order to navigate my transition from being in this world to being not of this world and a Kingdom-Minded Believer in Jesus, I hope that you will no longer feel alone as you face your Giants.

Nothing about this book is meant to establish Doctrine, nor is it meant to provide the reader with a step by step formula for "How To Succeed as a Christian". This book is simply my Testimony and my sharing of some of the most effective tools that the Lord equipped me with in order that maybe someone else would also be set free which would additionally redeem some of my past experiences. God is so good that as soon as we stop wrestling and give it to Him, He makes a way! He truly does "turn all things together for the good of those who love Him and are called according to His purposes ". (Romans 8:28) I believe that God has a purpose for each person, the question is "when will we say 'yes' to His Plan in our lives?" When will we jump up and down, yelling at the top of our lungs "pick me, pick me, pick me!"? Today is truly the acceptable Day of the Lord and it's a great day to step into who it is He's been calling you to become. Blessings over each and every one of you! May you encounter the

Fullness of His Grace and His Mercy as you travel along on your unique Journey with Him, in Jesus name I pray! Amen!

Introduction Disclaimer

The information that you are about to encounter within the pages of this book is not meant to be a recipe for someone else's success in their Christian walk. It is simply me choosing to share the Testimony of God's Amazing Grace in my life and what Jesus accomplished through His Gift of Salvation to me and how I then did my best to "walk it out" as led by the Holy Spirit.

The most important thing that I could share with you is the admonition that whatever information you find here, you should always take it back to Father God and see what it is that He wants you to know. The most important thing, I believe, is that each one of us works more and more each day to cultivate our ear to hear what Father God, Jesus, and the Holy Spirit want to share with us in each and every situation. Key questions are: Lord what does this mean, and, Lord what must I do?

Beginning to Write

I think that perhaps the hardest thing about writing a book is choosing where and how to start the book. It's almost as if you have to overcome the giant obstacle of: Wherever do I start?

Wisdom says that "they overcame by the Blood of the Lamb, the Word of their Testimony, and not loving their lives unto death" (Revelation 12:11). So in order to actually start writing, maybe what I will do is choose wisdom and share the Testimony of what the Lord Has done for me as I share some of the strategies that He has given me to overcome places where I found myself stuck in order to eventually, bit by bit, become the person He always made me to be.

That is how I shall begin...

Chapter 1: Leaning on My Own Understanding

As I share my Testimony with you, I am choosing to deliberately focus on what Father God was doing in my life, rather than give any undue credit to the enemy of my soul, satan. I do not feel that anything will be accomplished by highlighting the negative, rather, I choose to focus on the unending grace of the Lord as He persistently pursued me and watched over me even when I was making poor choices. I truly am convinced that His Grace is so much greater than we realize! It is only by the Grace of God that I am alive today, that much is certain.

Growing Up

Looking back on it, I feel that I grew up in the Lap of Luxury as well as in the Land of Entitlement. I went to a Preparatory School which is a fancy word for what they used to call Finishing Schools where they teach you all sorts of different things that are to equip you in life. It was actually a Grammar School and they specialized in teaching us how to write effectively which is a huge gift as I make my way through my life nowadays as a writer. However, what I remember most is that it was a really lonely place. You had to wear exactly the right clothes in order to be accepted or even spoken to and if you failed that test you were basically ostracized. Of course not having gotten that memo ahead of time, I showed up for the first day of 7th grade wearing my favorite pair of red plaid pants which immediately sent me to the Land of Losers. It took me until my senior year before I actually managed to sneak my way into No-Man's-Land where people basically tolerated you, but nobody ever went out of their way to include you amongst the privileged, popular ones. This actually served to give me some really great lessons in life because in reality, all we are is people that are confronted by the challenges that the world brings to us. Being adopted, I can say that one really interesting thing about people who have been adopted is that there's always a tendency to focus on what you didn't have, instead of focusing on the fact that you were actually chosen by someone and then given a far greater opportunity than you might have had otherwise. I think that points to the fallen nature of man, in that nothing is ever going to satisfy us until we get reconciled with the Lord.

What I knew of God back in those days boiled down to what I probably more than likely misunderstood from those moments when I was in Chapel during Parochial School. The person who was talking to us, also known as "Father", did not seem exceptionally happy nor did he seem very encouraging. In fact, he seemed a good bit angry and tended to speak using a loud voice that conveyed to me a good bit of anger and irritation at the general condition of those of us sitting in the pews.

What I knew of Jesus, on the other hand, was that He was loving and He embraced everyone because He loved everyone. I remember I used to really enjoy going to the Doctor's office because they had the Children's Bible there and I could read more about Jesus. He seemed nice. So when the time came for me to go to a Christian ski camp where in addition to skiing we did Bible studies and played Christian-themed games like Pictionary with Christian answers, I simply enjoyed the chance to learn more about Jesus. Skiing was a bonus. At the end of that week, they did a ceremony in which each youth in attendance was given the opportunity to invite Jesus into their heart. They did it in a non-threatening way as to whether or not we chose to receive Jesus. Once we had written down what our choice was, we were to fold up the piece of paper and quietly walk over and put it in the fire as a burnt offering. The question seem to be a no-brainer to me, of course I wanted more of Jesus in my life! Just thinking about Jesus made me feel good.

The challenge was learning what to do with my new decision to follow Christ and how to implement it within my life. Because when I returned home, there was no support system for me. We did not attend church and I did not have a Youth Group to go to or anyone to talk to about such things. So I guess it's not too surprising that I reverted to my old ways and that I bowed my knee to man's way of doing things. Throughout my childhood, all I had ever wanted was friends and it was pretty easy for me to be swayed by whatever my friends were doing and what they would think about my choices as to whether or not I joined them. I certainly didn't want to risk losing the few friends that I had. So, in a nutshell, within the course of two weeks I made the monumental choice of inviting Jesus into my life and then promptly turned my back on following Him and went back to my old way of conducting business which was… the world's way. Or to put it another way, I promptly set about cultivating an "authentic testimony" which would clearly demonstrate God's Grace and His overwhelming love for one who was lost in a momentous way!

Within the next couple of years, my closest friends begin attending Confirmation Class in order to be Confirmed within the denomination of worship which their parents had chosen. As a part of Confirmation Class there was a Youth Group and I used to love going to the Youth Group. Everything was going swimmingly and I was really enjoying the Youth Group until the week before our last session when I realized that, quite basically, I was not going to be able to be Confirmed because... I had never been Baptized. On the given day, I had to raise my hand and in front of the entire Youth Group explain that I was not going to be able to be Confirmed the following week. The Pastor also known as "Father", who was leading the Youth Group was clearly disappointed and he asked me "Why not?" I explained that I had never been Baptized. A look of joy came over his face and he said to me, "Oh that's wonderful! We could baptize you... We could baptize you at the local Country Club swimming pool! It would be wonderful!"

So I thought about it, and this is what I came up with: let's see, a great pool party, lots of friends, there's that new bathing suit I really like, oh and then there's Father God up in Heaven looking down at me next to a swimming pool with all the lightning bolts ever made right there next to Him in Heaven.

I didn't know much, but I sure did know "Fear of the Lord". I knew I wasn't ready to live my life the way I should. I also knew that God doesn't like hypocrites. And so in my immature mind, I put two and two together and I replied "No thank you, Sir. I just don't think I can do that."

You see, the denomination that I belonged to didn't really ever seem to discuss the depth of God's love for us. It didn't discuss His Grace. It didn't discuss the lengths to which He went to bridge the gap that man had created between us and God. And because of all those things, I chose to not take that next step within my Christian walk. I cannot say whether my choice was right or wrong, but I do feel that it reflected a certain amount of Integrity within my Spirit man.

Sadly, I had enough Integrity to know I didn't want to be a hypocrite, but not quite enough integrity to be willing to change and become who it was God wanted me to be.

A Snowball's Chance

Way back in the day, while I was still in High School, I took a notion late one night that I absolutely had to have a snowball. You know what I'm talking about, the snack cake that has a chocolate cake filled with cream, wrapped with pink marshmallow then topped off with coconut. Nothing else would do. So I hopped on my bike and rode the two miles down to the nearest convenience store in order to buy said snowball. After I got my treat, I was standing in line behind a guy when I slowly realized there was something odd going on. I couldn't quite put my finger on it for a couple minutes and then I suddenly realized: wait a minute, he's wearing a ski mask and it's pulled all the way down and this is only September! I casually looked around the side of him and discovered that: yes, he had a gun and it was pointed straight at the cashier! At that point in time, instead of performing in the heroic fashion which I would have liked to think I would have performed in, I found myself heading to the back of the store, saying quietly, "I think I'll check out the Twinkies ". I then hid behind the dairy case where I fervently prayed he would not steal my bike which I had left leaning up against the pole just inside the front door of the store.

After he left, I went up to the counter and talked to the clerk and said I was sorry I hadn't done more to help her to which she replied, "No, I think you did just fine." I then paid for my snowball and I left the actual scene of the crime.

I tell you this story in order to make a point: we tend to see ourselves in a certain way until we get put into a position where we learn that we are not the hero that we always thought we were, rather we find we have a strong instinct for survival!

The awesome thing about Father God is that He always sees us as He made us to be. He doesn't take note of our many micro failures on any given day, rather He sees the whole process and He sees who it is that we are becoming and He's happy that we have chosen to take the Journey with Him. What we need to do is learn how to focus on who it is He wants us to become and not get led astray by our notions of who we think we "should" be. That way we will arrive at the new us, and we will probably be eternally grateful for who it is that He made us to be and knew that we could be all along!

Isn't it exciting that the God of the Universe actually created us specifically in order to fulfill our role in His Master Plan? How cool is that?

The Spectrum of Belief

For as long as I can remember, I have been a "Believer". It is as if I have just always had an innate knowledge that God existed and that Jesus was who He said He was. I also believed the Church when they told me about the Holy Ghost and that all three members of the Godhead were the same God and that He was a living God. So in all senses of the word, I was a Believer. However, in retrospect, I was a nominal Believer. I believed in name only. I believed in the knowledge that I found within books concerning God and Jesus, as well as the knowledge that I was taught in Chapel and on Sundays within the four walls of the building of the Church. The fundamental aspect of Christianity that I was missing out on was the fullness of an encounter with the one true Living God.

Within the realm of Christianity, there are certain pivotal milestones which forever alter the way we see things. The first milestone would be the day that we come to believe that Jesus is the Son of God and that God exists. Another milestone occurs on the day that we get baptized as an expression of the way the Blood of Jesus and what He accomplished on the Cross washes us clean of our sins. Yet another milestone is the first time that we're baptized in the Holy Spirit and we receive all the gifts of the Spirit so that we are equipped to work out our salvation as we continue along on our journey of Christianity. One of the most significant milestones, I believe, is when we actually surrender our own self-will and truly make Jesus Christ the Lord of our Life. It is only when we do this that we can begin to be transformed into who it is that Father God is calling us to become - who it is He made us to be all along. Hand in hand with granting Jesus Lordship of our Life is the milestone of when we actually come to see our personal role in putting Him on the Cross. While it is true that we were not alive on planet Earth when the people voted to have Barabbas released and Jesus crucified, it is still also true that we are one of the reasons why Jesus was sent to Earth to die on the cross in order to make a way for man to have a relationship with Father God once again.

I actually believe that while Jesus was on the cross He lived or experienced every single person's entire life. When we look at the definition of sin, it becomes clear that any portion of our Lives that Jesus was not involved in and God was not a part of, was sin and Jesus *"took the sin of the world while he was on the cross"* (1 Peter 2:4). It's important for us to actually take a look at what that means. Unless we examine it, it is simply a euphemism for something that was excruciating because Jesus suffered and died so that we wouldn't have to. The Bible tells us that *"the wages of sin is death"* (Romans 6:23). No discussion. That is the standard. The Bible also tells us that all have *"fallen short of the glory of God"* (Romans 3:23). Not a single one of us passes the test, because if we break one rule we're guilty of breaking them all. This may seem like a harsh standard but that's a moot point-It's God's system not ours. It's not eternal life as defined by man, but rather God's plan to give man another opportunity to enter into the relationship of a lifetime as well as Eternity. *"For God so loved the world that He sent His only son that none should perish"* (John 3:16). So if the entire portion of our lives that we lived without God as the center of our lives is sin, then I believe that Jesus experienced all of that on the Cross. Once we invite Him into our lives, He says He'll *"never leave us nor forsake us"* (Hebrews 13:5) therefore, He lives that portion of our lives as well.

I believe that Jesus experienced every single anguishing moment that each one of us has lived through, every single bad thing that was ever done to us, every single bad thing that we ever did, and He also experienced being wrongfully accused of all those horrible things that we did in our lives that fell short of the glory of God. As He was experiencing these things, He knew what the position of our hearts was. When He said *"forgive them, they know not what they do"* (Luke 23:34), He said it as our friend because He knew us through and through after having experienced the entirety of our lives while He was on the Cross. The Bible tells us *"no greater gift than a man lay down his life"* (John 15:13-17) for a friend. Since Jesus lived the entirety of our lives out while upon the Cross, He is well aware of what Father God's Plan is for our lives and therefore He is eminently qualified to be the Lord of our life, giving us good guidance in all circumstances. When we yoke our minds to the mind of Christ, we have access to the solutions of Heaven!

There's such a thing as a Decorator Crab. In order to disguise itself from predators, it affixes different tidbits that are left on the bottom of the ocean to its shell. In doing so, it confuses any predators which might be looking for a quick meal. The more it decorates itself, the more it blends in with the bottom of the ocean and the safer it would seem to be. I believe there are some Christians who truly do believe in God, His son Jesus

Christ, and maybe even in the Holy Spirit, but they still want to be liked within the world. They still want to live a life of anonymity within the world, blending in as it were, just like the Decorator Crab. This is exceptionally dangerous and usually does not end well. God says that He would rather a person be either hot or cold, not lukewarm because He will "spew" them out of His mouth (Revelation 3:16). God also says that you can only serve one master because a house divided amongst itself will fall (Mark 3:24). Anytime we compromise God's standard and try to blend in with the world, we are dividing our own house and we are going to fall.

Jesus Himself told us that because the world hated Him first, it would hate us as well (John 15:18). Jesus tells us that He has chosen us out of the world and therefore we are no longer of the world (John 15:19), therefore the world will not embrace us because we no longer belong. We need to take a stand, especially since Jesus said *"If you deny me in front of man, I will deny you in front of my father"* (Matthew 10:33) … I don't know about you, but I don't ever want Jesus to deny me. Without Him I would be oh so lost and I would have absolutely no hope.

High School Revisited

When I went back for my 15-year High School Reunion, each and every person I spoke with indicated that they too were miserable during those years of High School.

Who would have guessed? Most of them were the truly popular people. And I really thought that they had the world by the tail back in those days so to speak. In reality though, they all confessed to being thoroughly miserable during the High School years. Some of this I believe is due to each and every one of us trying to make our way and figure out who it was that we actually were while coming into agreement with all of the crazy hormones that were flowing. I think that that section of our lives is just always a difficult adjustment.

Learning About Leadership

When I joined the military, there was a whole new level of adjustment required. The majority of that adjustment concerned learning how to be a Team Player. I think I was better equipped for this than most because the whole concept of the military was so far removed from what my life had been up to that point that it didn't take much to convince me that I definitely could not do everything on my own and succeed. So I quickly converted to being a Team Player and that was actually further established in my understanding as I went through some of the Schools that I then attended in order to get me ready for the military "pipeline" established for my particular area of service. One of the tremendous benefits to realizing that you cannot accomplish all things on your own and that you need help from others is that it opens your eyes to understand that each one of us is: simply a person.

Those who find themselves in positions of leadership are not necessarily always the best qualified for it. In some instances, those who make their way to the top of the heap (at least within the military), are actually those who have never ever gone out on a limb and taken a huge chance in order to accomplish something phenomenal within their career. Since they never choose to take a risk, generally speaking, they are not likely to fail in an epic fashion. Within the military, it's quite common that out of 10 assignments, a person might epically fail in one yet that's the one thing that is remembered about their career rather than the nine times that they accomplished phenomenal, borderline miracles within their field of endeavor. That seemed to be the quintessential challenge of being known as a "Shell Answer Man" within the military; the more times people come up to you with challenging requests, the greater the odds of you letting someone down. All in all though, my military experience really opened my eyes to understand that **man is man, he is not God**, and he never will be. (Hallelujah!) As people, we are all equals - it's the Holy Spirit that gives us an edge - this is why it's so important for us to take each thing that people tell us back to God in order to see what it is that He would have us know in each instance.

Within my life, coming back to the Lord and beginning to truly walk with Him was a process. It was almost an inch by inch process as He wooed me, always demonstrating the depths of His Love for me even when I was not walking with Him or allowing Him to be the Lord of my life. As I look back on those days when I truly was lost and at a loss for what I could do in order to become the person I wanted to be, I can see His hand in my life at all times! It seemed that whenever I made the right choice and did the right thing, there was always an almost immediate reward, a Blessing so to speak. A good example of this is the way He never let go of me despite the wrong choices I was making. In my twenties I mistakenly tried to win friends by being the life of the party so to speak. All that this really accomplished was me giving away my self-respect bit by bit to where some days it was really difficult to look at myself in the mirror. I was living in an area at the time where no matter where you went you always had to drive a good distance to get there as well as to get home. In short, it didn't take rocket science to realize that sooner or later I was going to be stopped for Driving Under the Influence.

Since I was in the military at the time, I ended up experiencing what can really only be described as Double Jeopardy - I had to fulfill the requirements within the civilian legal system as well as those within the Military and what this meant was that I got graded down in my "Judgment as an Officer" because, quite frankly, it's poor judgment to drive a car after you've been drinking. I was able to what we call "white-knuckle it" and just not drink for about 6 months and then I pretty much was right back to where I'd started. There were a bunch of us who would meet at the bar right outside the gates of the Base and we would hang out there until "traffic calmed down". Well, that was a recipe for disaster. So, unfortunately by my continued bad choices, I ended up getting a second DUI within the three-year probationary period of the first DUI. As a result, part of my civilian sentencing afforded me the "opportunity" to attend Alcohol Awareness Education. The amazing thing in this whole episode was that the Military never found out and so I didn't suffer that double jeopardy a second time.

In the beginning, I looked on the Alcohol Awareness Education as a significant pain in the neck mixed with a blessing in that I was still allowed to drive my car to and from work and to fulfill the requirements of my civilian sentence. No pleasure driving though. I was exceedingly grateful that the Military did not find out. Had my license been revoked, it would have been a different story for sure! As a part of the Alcohol Awareness Education Program, we all signed a pledge to not drink alcohol for the duration of the curriculum. To be honest, most of the people who were attending the Alcohol Awareness Education were still drinking even though we had all agreed to the terms and signed the pledge that we were not going to drink during the 18 months of this education.

The program that I was in required weekly class sessions, and every other week we had to meet individually with our counselor, and every other week there was a group session for us to attend and throughout the whole process we had to be going to weekly AA meetings. The interesting thing is that I had really been wanting to stop drinking, but I just had no idea how to do it. I know that sounds funny because in reality, all you do is **you just don't drink**. It's not that complex. However, the friends who I had cultivated were all avid drinkers because that's what we tend to do; we tend to surround ourselves by people who are like us so that we can be comfortable about who it is that we are. So I kept making agreements with myself whereby "I will quit after this next party", and it just had really gotten like a roller coaster ride. It wasn't that I had to drink every day to excess; it was just that when I did let myself drink I was definitely drinking too much. One of the best summaries of this type of approach to drinking that I ever heard was this: one is too many and a million is not enough. That's just the kind of girl I was. Plus when I would drink, I would just want to do outrageous things like rappel down the outside of a building from balcony to balcony or something equally stupid but it "sure did seem like a good idea at the time." Like I said... Life of the party.

Well one day I realized: What if this is God giving me a way to stop drinking? Him holding His hand down to me from Heaven with the answer I have been searching for? What if I just tell all my friends that while I'm in this program I'm not allowed to drink? That takes it off of me having to explain to them why and it takes it off of them having to examine their own drinking habits. What tends to happen is that if I have a group of friends who I routinely drink with and I suddenly realize that I have a problem with drinking or am even an alcoholic, that forces them to have to take a look at their own drinking habit and they don't want to do that. So they all try to convince you, or me in this case, that I don't have a problem and that I could just come back to drinking with them and everything would be fine. Not the case.

The awesome thing is that as soon as I made the decision to accept the help that God was offering to me, and I reached out and grabbed a hold of His promise, **I was set free**. He completely delivered me from any desire whatsoever to drink. So much so that I can't even give people rides who have been drinking because the mere smell of the alcohol coming out of their pores actually gives me the dry heaves! That can only be God! The fact that I went from loving drinking to actually physically retching when I encounter the scent of alcohol is truly a miracle.

As I went through the 18-month Alcohol Awareness Education Program I learned a lot. I learned about the devastating effects of drinking over a prolonged period of time. I also learned about the different ways alcoholism can manifest, in that it's not so much how much you drink, sometimes the determining factor is what do you do when you cannot get a drink. So there are a lot of ins and outs to it. But God was so good that He completely took that burden away from me. After about three years, I no longer even went to AA Meetings. The reason I chose to no longer go to those meetings was because I no longer needed to talk about alcohol whatsoever because it's not a part of my reality whatsoever. I don't have alcohol in my home. I don't ingest alcohol in food. I don't even like using a mouthwash that has alcohol because I honestly don't know what might ever possibly trigger me to want alcohol again and although I know that I may have a whole lot of more drunken moments in me, and I also know for sure that I don't know if I have another straight. I don't know that I could make it out of that maze again. Please don't misunderstand, I'm simply talking about my own experience in life. I am not saying that my path is the path that any other human being should ever consider taking. I am certain you have your own path and that you hear from God and that you are walking with Him day by day guiding you. One of the great benefits of the AA program is that it encourages people to examine themselves Spiritually. As I worked my way through that process, I ended up having an ever greater relationship with the Lord through praying to Him on a nightly basis and talking to Him at the end of each day and going through my day and seeing what things I might have been able to do better in the hopes that the next time I would do better. I took that time in my life to get to know myself better and to try to better understand what the motivators were in my life.

I realized that one of the biggest motivations in my life had been the desire to have friends. I just wanted to know that there were people who cared about me. Even people who loved me. I don't know why but for some reason we tend to discount the love that our parents have for us by saying "Well, you have to love me - you're my Mom or my Dad." As if somehow their love doesn't count. That's a lie straight from the pit of Hell. In fact, most of our parents would go through Hell for us if they thought that it would help us. The same way Jesus gave His life so that we could spend eternity with Him when we choose to receive that great gift of Salvation from Him.

Baptized by His Agape Love

Shortly after I returned home from one of my regular visits with my mom, I was reading a book that was very interesting. In the early pages of the book, the main character had gone to get some beer from a convenience store. As she left the store, a group of men stopped her and demanded her money from her. One of the people within the group had a chokehold on her that was so significant she could not get her hand out of her pocket with the money and she began to lose consciousness because she couldn't breathe. So she called on Heaven and Heaven responded by a bright white light coming straight down from Heaven to touch her! As it touched her, it gave her the energy to remove her hand with the money in it from her pocket and break free from her captor who quite happily took her money and the beer and left. As soon as I read this, and learned that Heaven responded to people, I said out loud: "I want to see that!" That was basically it. No huge prayer. No reverential moment. No begging God to demonstrate Himself to me. Just the fervent response of my heart crying out loud: "I want to see that!"

The very next day, I was driving over to an undeveloped area where I often walked my dogs. I was waiting at a red light when all of the sudden Heaven opened and a bright white light came down from Heaven, went through the top of my pickup truck and entered in through the top of my head, filling me to overflow with the pure Agape Love that only God offers. I was amazed!

The first thing that happened was I heard myself saying out loud: "If no one on Earth ever loves me again, it doesn't matter because God loves me!" The next thing I said out loud was: "If we could just bottle this there would be no more war... until we ran out." And my final thought out loud was: "I really ought to call and ask Mom if she wants to come and live with me."

Don't misunderstand me, I loved my mother very much and had a great relationship with her from a distance. However, when we were in the same house it was clear there were too many cooks in the kitchen. Sometimes parents have difficulty seeing that their children are grown, and they also don't really know how to interact with their children once they are grown especially if the child moved away at a relatively early age. Since I left home right after graduating from college and moved all the way across the country and then was in the Military, my mom didn't really know how to interact with me at that level. My mom was also a good bit older since she had adopted me when she was 47 years old... Talk about a change in life!

What strikes me about the encounter I had is several things. I was not walking with God at the time, in fact, I was marching to my very own beat and was smoking pot since I was no longer in the Military. I had not smoked any pot at the time of this encounter though because I had just returned from traveling all the way across the country. The next thing that strikes me about this encounter is that, if God would do that in His pursuit of me, He wants to do that in His pursuit of all of His children. He wants all of us to understand just how much He Loves us. When I experienced the bright white light of His Love, it was clear! There was no longer any question about it -The God who breathed the Universe into existence Loved me with a never-ending Love!

I never shared this encounter with anyone because, first and foremost, it was extremely personal and I didn't want anyone to take anything away from it by calling it into question. I was keenly aware that it was a significant moment and I did not think that it was a common occurrence. I was pretty sure that if things like that happened on a regular basis somebody would have been talking about it somewhere.

The other reason why I never shared this encounter is because I knew based upon my Yankee upbringing, that "It is far better to keep your mouth shut and let people think you're an idiot, rather than open your mouth and confirm the fact!" I also had a bit of a suspicion that my friends who all smoked pot with me would probably be convinced that I had some really, really good stuff and they might actually ransack my house trying to find it because I didn't think that they would believe that it was just a "God" thing. However, I'm here to tell you He is just that much in love with you! And He wants to show you how much He loves you right now, today, so I ask:

Father God, I am asking that what you did for me you will do for the reader right now, in Jesus' Name, that you will touch them from the top of their head all the way down to the bottoms of their feet and reveal to them the depth of your love to them so that they would never, ever, ever wonder again. I thank you Lord for your great love for each one of your Sons and Daughters. And I thank you that you are an all-consuming fire and that as they come to know your great love for them, they will be consumed with a fiery passion for you, in Jesus' Name I pray. Amen.

The Opportunity of a Lifetime

About 12 years after the Lord delivered me from my desire to drink, my Mom asked me to come for a visit since my brother would also be in town and she wanted help clearing out some of the stuff from the house as she was getting older. She had been given the diagnosis of Parkinson's and was trying to take care of some of the things that would need to be taken care of while she could still help. Near the end of my time there on that visit, my brother and I were standing in the backyard talking about Mom and I very clearly heard the audible voice of God ask me "At what point does someone who is as independent as she is ask for help?" So I turned to my brother and I told him that if Mom was alright with it, I could move up and help her while living in one of the houses that she had been renting out to others. When I asked Mom how she felt about that idea, she got the most beautiful smile on her face that I had ever seen. So I packed up all my stuff into one bedroom of the house that I owned and then offered to let a friend of mine live in my house rent free while taking care of my dogs and I moved to be with my Mom. In order to preserve my sanity while trying to help my Mom who was struggling with receiving help because she was so independent, I started attending the AA Meetings down at the bottom of the street we lived on. It offered a good forum for me to make friends with people who had a similar focus and was also a safe place for me to dump some of the stuff that I just couldn't carry. One of the great things about AA is that when you share something absolutely wretched, nobody there ever passes judgment on you, and in fact 8 out of 10 people will come up to you afterwards and say: "well that was really nothing compared to the horrific things that I did." It takes away the shame. It also helps you feel that you're not all alone trying to make your way.

At this point in time I was still convinced that most of the people sitting within the Church pews were hypocrites so I was not actively pursuing going to Church. AA seemed like the best alternative for me at that point in my life. Mom had her ups and downs and a little over two years after I moved up to be with her, she suffered a blood clot to her lungs and died. Once again God's grace was sufficient, because the night before she died, I was prompted by the Holy Spirit to whisper in her ear how much I loved her and that I could have never hoped to have such a great mom as her and that I would miss her every day for the rest of my life. The Lord also caused one of the Nurses at the Hospital to realize that Mom was passing and so she sat with my Mom and held her hand as she passed. God is so Good!

Ever since moving back to be with my Mom, I had been quite open with her and had told her that I knew beyond any question of a doubt that "God exists." Unfortunately, at that particular time in my life I did not understand how vital Jesus is to the equation, and so I did not offer Mom the real key to Salvation. Oddly enough though, I had at one point actually laid hands on her and concentrated on feeling the peace that God had given me one night, and so without knowing what I was doing, I had tried to impart peace beyond all understanding to Mom through the laying on of hands and she immediately calmed down. God is so good! Even when I was not walking with Him or allowing Him to be the Lord of my life, He was still blessing others through me. It astounds me when I think about it!

My Christian Reawakening

Shortly after my Mother passed away, I met a man who talked non-stop about Jesus and how Jesus was the only way to the Father. Up to this point, my walk with the Lord had been one of considering all three members of the Trinity as coming under the address of "Lord". I always knew God was real and believed that Jesus had existed and walked the earth as a man and that the Holy Ghost also existed, although I have to admit I didn't much know what to do with the Holy Ghost. Little was said about the Holy Ghost in the few services I had ever attended. As I considered Jesus, I knew that I had invited Him into my heart many years earlier which had opened up the possibility of a relationship with all three members of the Trinity. Apparently the time had come to start learning more about this Christianity thing. Here are some of the new truths I learned along the way as I came alive to Christianity.

Jesus is The Way, The Truth, and The Life!

Jesus is the only door through whom we can enter into a relationship with Father God. The Holy Spirit is the gift which allows us to actually walk out our salvation in power and Grace. Until we are filled with the Holy Spirit, the Bible is perplexing to us; it is foolishness to those who are perishing (1 Corinthians 1:18). It is only through the gift of the Holy Spirit that we can begin to understand God's word as the Holy Spirit will lead us in all truth (John 16:13). By the guidance of the Holy Spirit, we are actually able to renew our minds which transforms us (Romans 12:2) into who we were always made to be. Jesus redeems our created worth and the Holy Spirit transforms us as we are truly freed from the entanglements of our fallen world. In this way, we can learn how to be in the world without being of the world (John 17:14) which would cause us to be at odds with God for you cannot serve two masters (Matthew 6:24) and will be at emnity with God until you allow yourself to be sanctified and set apart for His use.

Jesus serves as our example of how to overcome the world. He continually invites us to "follow me". He leads us by example and continuously lavishes the Father's Love on us as He guides us into ever-increasing harmony with the Father's Heart. He was always in constant communion with His Father, always looking to see what His Father was doing and praying unceasingly. He sought out quiet moments alone with His Father and we should as well. After Jesus was baptized, the Holy Spirit came down in bodily form like a dove and then led Him out into the Wilderness to fast and pray, spending time with His Father, worshipping Him in spirit and in truth. The key is that the Holy Spirit led Him to the Wilderness. I believe that when satan came to tempt Jesus, the Holy Spirit facilitated His ability to overcome the temptations. God always provides a way out when we are tempted (1 Corinthians 10:13). We need to follow Jesus's example as we navigate the temptations within our own lives. We need to use the Bible as our manual for how to overcome the world by seeking out how God sees us to be and His promises for who He wants to be for us. We need to then speak and declare those promises over our lives as we overcome the world following Jesus who is our Lord and Savior.

The Extravagant Love of The Father

God had a plan all along. He made Adam for fellowship; He made him in His own image (Genesis 1:26) and walked with him in the cool of the day in the Garden of Eden. He made woman to complete Adam and be a companion to him (Genesis 2:18). In the garden, God tasked Adam and Eve to be fruitful and multiply (Genesis 1:28). He allowed them to eat from every tree except the Tree of the Knowledge of Good and Evil, warning them that surely they would die on the day that they ate of it (Genesis 2:16). That command was actually designed to protect Adam and Eve from the wages of sin which is death (Romans 6:23). When the serpent questioned Eve about the command, she actually added to it, claiming God said they would die if they even touched the fruit.

After Adam and Eve allowed doubt to creep in and fell to temptation in the garden, God's first response was not anger. He called out to them asking where they were and when they admitted that they were hiding because they were ashamed of their nakedness (Genesis 3:7), God simply asked who had told them they were naked (Genesis 3:11)? The first consequence God handed out was to satan and in reality it was a reiteration of man's authority over satan. God proclaimed that the offspring of

Eve would crush the head of the serpent (Genesis 3:15). Additional consequences occurred, however, it is important to realize that our Heavenly Father acted in a loving and compassionate way despite His disappointment in man. Father God even ensured that there could be no access to the Tree of Life (Genesis 3:24) until after Jesus redeemed Man by paying the price for man's transgressions.

The Naked Truth

Since they had just eaten from the Tree of Knowledge of Good and Evil, Adam and Eve knew what they did was disobedient and they knew that He knows everything. So their disobedience was clearly evident, there was no hiding it; they were exposed in their disobedience - also known as naked. The Naked Truth was: they allowed doubt to enter their relationship with God. They chose to be disobedient. They were facing the consequences for their actions.

From the very moment we learned we were naked and out-of-place, we began clothing ourselves with layer upon layer upon layer of whatever we could put our hands on. The problem is the what was readily available was worldly. It was never meant for us. It didn't fit, but we still covered ourselves with it to try to blend in. Even if that worked for a time, we always knew it wasn't right for us. On some deep, deep, deep level, we knew it wasn't for us and we were uncomfortable with in our own skin. The problem is that no one else talked about it. No one else shared their discomfort and so we figured we were "the only one" ... the only misfit.

Deep down, all we ever wanted was to feel like we belonged; like we were appreciated for who we were; like we were loved! The good news is that you are loved - you always have been! The very one who breathed the Universe into existence, lovingly formed you to be exactly who you are deep down - exactly as He made you to be. The challenge is that the layers of what you have clothed yourself with - and the disappointments life served up on your behalf - and the shame you were made to feel, all that needs to go! That really is good news! The challenge is: you are going to feel naked once again! Naked in front of the Lord. Yes, it is time to unmask yourself and allow Him to help you come clean so you can begin to allow your mind to be renewed and transformed by the washing of the word. It is time to allow yourself to become the new creation you were always meant to be - for if any man be in Christ, he is a new creation, all things are made new... ALL THINGS! (2 Corinthians 5:17)

You were made in the very image of the most high God - in His likeness so that as you are transformed from glory to glory, when others look upon you they see Him! They see the Light of the World! They see the one who captivates our hearts! They see the One we lay down our lives for - the Firstborn of many Sons - and it is time for the Sons of God to be revealed for all the Earth is groaning for the appearance of the Sons of God! So it is time to let Him peel away the layers of camouflage and self-deception, the masks of apathy, and allow the Son of Glory to be reflected by you in all that you do and say as you receive His Robe of Righteousness in exchange for those coverings which simply do not fit. Let Him shed His grace upon you that you may be a carrier of His glory and lives maybe transformed, one heart at a time, according to His great Plan through the gift of His loving Son, Jesus Christ!

In the wilderness after Moses led the Israelites out of Egypt with God's assistance, it soon became clear that the people needed Godly guidelines. The Lord gave Moses the Ten Commandments (Exodus 20). Since the Lord knows all of the secrets of our hearts (Psalms 44:20), He undoubtedly knew that man would not succeed in keeping the Commandments. God knew that Moses would not even succeed in bringing the Commandments down the mountain without breaking them physically as well as spiritually by allowing his anger to overcome him upon discovering what the Israelites had been up to while he was on the mountain receiving the Commandments. God has known the true heart of man all along (1 Kings 8:39), yet He loves us anyway and has given everything to reach us through His Son, Jesus, who overcame sin and through whom all men may receive salvation through the victory that Jesus accomplished on the Cross at Calvary (John 3:16).

By the time Jesus walked the Earth, there were over 600 laws governing life in Jewish Society, and if a person broke one of them they were considered to have broken them all (James 2:10). There were so many requirements that it was virtually impossible to memorize them all, let alone observe them. Jesus, however, fulfilled all the requirements and all the Commandments and was accorded righteousness by His Father, God. *"For Christ is the end of the law for righteousness to everyone who believes"* (Romans 10:4). Because of this, Jesus was able to serve as a spotless and sin-free sacrifice (1 Peter 1:19) to atone for the sins of all of mankind. While walking on Earth as the Son of Man and actively discipling others, Jesus exemplified the requirements of living a Godly life by demonstrating the utmost importance of Love. He stated that the two most important Commandments were: to love the Lord your God with all your heart, soul and mind and to love your neighbor as yourself (Matthew 22:37). He declared that the world would know that they were his disciples by the way they loved one another (John 13:35)!

Father God's extravagant Love prompted Him to send His son, Jesus, that He might die for us. Jesus atoned for our sins that we would have life more abundant (John 10:10)! Imagine that: death led to everlasting life! Satan thought he had won when Jesus was on the Cross, however as the veil was torn within the Temple and Jesus completed His assignment on the Cross, it became clear that satan had actually played right into God's hands and yet another Covenant had been established. A Blood Covenant, sealed with the precious Blood of Jesus, the ultimate sacrifice. It was written in "stone" because Christ is The Rock that Christianity is founded upon.

The Bible tells us that God will use the foolish to confound the wise (1 Corinthians 1:27). satan thought he had everything figured out and that he should be worshipped in the place of God. satan thought that his plan had succeeded only to realize that God had prevailed and that through dying, Jesus had birthed life Eternal! God is extravagant and His Word is Eternal. He wants all of His Sons and Daughters to partner with Him as Heaven invades Earth. He wants His church, Jesus Christ's Bride, to show how foolish and truly powerless the princes and principalities of this world really are. God is taking those in society who are considered lost, the last and the least, and placing them first (Matthew 20:16) as He gives us an upgrade by bringing us into our rightful position as Sons and Daughters and Co-Heirs with Christ (Romans 8:17). All that the Lord requires is the activation of our faith - step into it, get in motion, let Him direct you through the Holy Spirit as you partner with Him and His will is done on Earth as it is in Heaven.

God knows that these are "End Days" and He knows exactly what He placed in each and every person He ever created. He saved the best for last and we were all made for a time such as this! He knows what we are all capable of as well as what He has specifically created us for (Ephesians 2:10). All of the circumstances that He has brought you through were actually designed to qualify you to reach another and set them free in the Name of Jesus!

Release the Kingdom wherever you go by activating your faith and demonstrating the power of His Love in your life!

In summary, the Good News is: He loves us! We have been forgiven. He wants us to walk with Him. He made us so He could love us. Jesus paid for ALL the sins of mankind (1 John 2:2). He is faithful and He has forgiven us (Luke 23:34). He has given us all authority in the Name of Jesus to walk in dominion as we release the kingdom, enforcing the victory Jesus Christ of Nazareth won on the Cross at Calvary!

Free Will

Basically everything comes down to choice and free will. God has given man free will because God wants to know that we choose Him. So our choice while we are in the land of the living down here on earth comes down to a choice between God's way or the world's way. Another way to look at it is it comes down to a choice between the two trees that were first talked about back in the Garden of Eden - the Tree of the Fruit of the Knowledge of Good and Evil and the Tree of Life. Sometimes we need to step back from a situation and consider what it is that we think we are in need of? Are we trying to gain information or knowledge for knowledge's sake and if we are, we need to realize that we are actually choosing to eat from the Tree of the Knowledge of Good and Evil and that does not end well.

The Currency of Heaven

God's currency is faith. The Bible tells us on many different occasions that it is impossible to please God without faith. (Hebrews 11:6) God wants to know that we trust Him. He wants to know that we have truly made His son, Jesus Christ, the Lord of our life. He wants to know in every single situation that we choose God, His way, and Life over man, the world's way, and Death. When we consider our choices in light of this information, it seems to make the choice a whole lot simpler in my opinion. I would always choose Life over Death. I would always choose God's way over the world's way because I have seen the devastation that the world wreaks upon people who are unsuspecting and do not know the fullness of the Spiritual War that they are caught right up in the middle of. In addition to these things, I also know that God is a masterful mathematician and I know that when I invest in Him, there is such an incredible multiplication in the fruit that is harvestable afterwards, that it is stunning. So I choose to follow Jesus. I choose to place my trust in God. And I choose to invest my faith in His Supernatural Kingdom, knowing that what He's bringing forth is far greater than anything I could ever even begin to imagine!

Once we have given our hearts to Jesus by asking Him to be our Lord and savior, there should begin to be a change in our lives. There should be something different about us. It is only by the Grace of God that we are saved (Ephesians 2:8) and we should never begin to think that we played any role in our own salvation; salvation is never due to any "good deed" that we may have done, it is only by the grace of God that we are granted salvation. We are only righteous in Jesus (Romans 3:22) once we have accepted Him as our Lord and Savior. However, now that we have been saved, our new faith in Jesus should begin to become evident through new behavior in our lives.

As the Holy Spirit convicts us of areas in our lives where we need to change our way of conducting ourselves, we begin to be transformed by the renewing of our minds (Romans 12:2) and a new way of living our lives develops. As our faith is activated, there should be a radical change in the way we see ourselves as well as in the way we lead our lives. There will be a shift from living in a manner that is self-focused (sinful) to living as a new creation where we prefer others above ourselves (Romans 12:10) and we become ambassador's for Christ and ministers of reconciliation (2 Corinthians 5:18) who walk in love which covers a multitude of sins (1 Peter 4:8).

Testing in the Wilderness

As new Christians, it's important to realize that there will be trials where our resolve to live in a new way will be tested and we will be tempted to return to old, comfortable behavior patterns. Remember, Jesus Himself was led by the Holy Spirit Into the Wilderness to be tempted by satan. Scripture defeated the enemy. The most effective way to defeat doubt is to counter it directly with scriptural truth, just as Jesus did. He is our model for success in all matters and since we are seated in Heavenly places in Christ Jesus (Ephesians 2:6), we always have access to Heaven's solution for any dilemma we may face. God will never allow us to be tempted without providing a solution to our situation (1 Corinthians 10:13). God wants each of His children to succeed, to excel, especially in the area of Scriptural Warfare. I believe He wants to know that we are willing to fight the Christian fight as we stand firm upon our Rock of Salvation, Jesus Christ. God wants us to step into who He made us to be, fully knowing who we are in Christ so that we may fight as we undo the works of the enemy, standing firm upon our inheritance through Jesus' victory on the Cross. We are to enforce His victory upon the Cross as we advance His Kingdom on Earth as it is in Heaven (Matthew 6:10).

Just know that you're never alone. **Never!** I believe each one of us goes through our own season of learning that the Church and man can only offer us a minimum semblance of what it is that we need from God. In reality, He really is the only one who Loves us the way He Loves us and He's the only one who could ever Love us in the way that we need to be Loved and that's because He knows us through and through and He knows just what we need.

The Love Languages

One of our biggest challenges (I believe) is learning how to express love in a way that can be received by another. There are five different love languages according to the experts who have studied this, and this could very well be the beginning of our dilemma. The Bible tells us to treat others as we would be treated (Luke 6:31), however, if my personal love language is different than yours then you may not recognize that the things I do for you are a demonstration of love because they may not actually be what you would like me to do for you. For example, if I clean up the reading area but you then are unable to find your important papers, have I really helped you? Or if I wash your car but you desire quality time as a demonstration of love, you might never realize how much I love and value you.

I believe that just as Father God wants to know each of His children, we each are born with an innate desire to be known and loved for who we are. The best gift we can give another is to actually take the time and effort to learn their specific love language – is it: quality time, acts of service, words of affirmation, a gentle touch, or a thoughtful gift?

I believe that when the Lord instructs us to *"do unto others as we would have done unto us"* (Luke 6:31 and Matthew 7:12), it is actually an invitation for us to invest in developing a Kingdom relationship with another. His desire is for us to know others and be known as we encourage each other to become who we have always wanted to be, perfected and wholly healed in Him!

Receiving Love and Loving Well

On the simplest of all levels, we need to remember:

If it is negative or past tense, it is of or from satan. He is the father of ALL lies. The very opposite of a lie is the Truth, so...Flip it and Flip it good! Therefore, if he whispers or shouts that you are a loser and all alone and what you are doing does not matter, the TRUTH IS: You are a WINNER, surrounded by Heaven's Host and Each and Every thing you do COUNTS for God's Kingdom!!!!

While I was spending time with the Lord one day, I realized that if I have these periodic moments of feeling like I'm all alone and don't really have any friends, suddenly being known and having a lot of people know who I am and wanting to interact with me would only make me that much more insecure. In other words, it would be like the Celebrity Syndrome, where you suddenly find yourself wondering why people want to spend time with you - what's in it for them? - and it would just make the aloneness that much more pronounced. I realized I do not want a platform. I want a close group of friends whom I trust and who are like-minded and want to walk life out alongside one another, going on assignment for the Lord. I only want to be known by those I have interacted with. I do not want a name. I want to go by Faith! I would far rather be known in heaven than on Earth.

At the end of the day, I actually found myself thinking about my mom who has been gone for quite a few years. I remembered how she always did her best to let me know that she loved me and appreciated me and respected me and really cherished me. Unfortunately, at the time I always put it off to the concept of "of course you have to say you love me cuz you're my mother". I now realize that she really did the best she could with what she had and I also now know that those who've never really been shown or taught how to love are only able to give out what it is they've been given or show love in the way that love was shown to them. She grew up in a generation where it was enough to have provided a good house and a good family and good opportunities for someone, but where there was no real talk defining what it means to love someone or how you show that you love someone. She was a twin and that in and of itself raises significant challenges. How tough would it be to not have a really good estimation of your own self worth and to then look and see someone who looks just like you receiving the accolades that you so long for in your own life? That would just be really, really, really tough to get beyond.

In short, we all battle our own version of insecurity and none of us knows the fight going on inside of another person, that is why it's so important for us to encourage one another and build one another up in love. Sometimes just demonstrating that someone is worthy of saying "hello" to is huge to that person. That's one of the reasons why we never know what the effect is going to be of our simple actions on others. Another reason is that we might pause and hesitate because we would be overwhelmed by our potential to mess things up. In either event, the good news is Love Never Fails and so if we just continue to demonstrate love and treat others with honor and respect and humility, hopefully we will each finish our race well.

Old Testament Christianity vs The Kingdom of God

While there is a lot of value found within the Old Testament, such as the amazing history of God's never ending pursuit of reconciliation with man, leaving Christianity at an Old Testament place where God is still "angry with man" is a very dangerous thing to do. When we choose the route of continuously threatening Hellfire and Damnation to the "Unsaved", we run the risk of failing in our mission. Jesus Himself called it the Good News. What kind of a witness to the goodness of God are we projecting when we are forever simply threatening others using a "You Had Better Come Around to Seeing it Our Way or Else" Model? What hope do we release into their lives? What practical strategies are we giving them for becoming victorious within their lives today?

The problem with the Old Testament "Hellfire and Damnation" Model of Christianity is that it leaves Jesus on the Cross. It is all about stressing the fact that man has no hope, that he is doomed to eternity in Hell with no way to help himself. It doesn't emphasize what it is that Jesus accomplished on the Cross! When we only focus on mankind's inability to help himself without sharing the Good News of what God did for us through the gift (John 3:16) of His own Son, Jesus, it would almost seem that we are partnering with Satan (whether we realize it or not) because we're certainly focusing on what satan accomplished as he introduced doubt to the heart of mankind in the Garden and then even inspired God's chosen people to turn against His Son, Jesus, when they elected to have a known murderer released and Jesus crucified (Mark 15).

We need to explain the importance of the Cross while at the same time praising God for making a way for each and every one of us to enter in to a relationship with Him (John 10:9). What a tragedy it is when we only share the negative portion of the message and we neglect to let people know that what Jesus did on the Cross over 2000 years ago was enough to cover them as well, if they only choose to receive Him as their Lord and Savior!

May He meet you right in the middle of your moment. May you look up, and turn, and see Him standing there with

His arms wide open, waiting, just waiting, for you to notice Him. May you wrap yourself in Him, and never be the same again, in Jesus' Name I pray! Amen!

Some Truth About satan

satan is a created being. Note the use of the present tense; satan is real. He was created along with all the other angels for the purpose of worshiping God. He was created in such a way that as he moved about Heaven performing his daily tasks, he actually made music. He then entered into rebellion by deciding that he should be worshipped just as God was. In fact, he decided that he would establish his own throne above God. Jesus tells us that He saw Satan "fall like lightning from Heaven". Ever since then, satan has taken it as his direct mission to do whatever he can to steal, kill and destroy those of us who were handmade by Father God in God's likeness with the potential of bearing the image of Father God. Yes, that's right, man was made in the likeness of God to bear His image. As we allow Jesus to transform us, we look more and more like God. This does not make us our own God, rather it makes us heirs of Salvation if we choose to receive the gift that Jesus has offered us through what He accomplished on the Cross.

What happened in the garden was far deeper than man simply choosing to eat forbidden fruit. What happened was that satan introduced doubt into man's heart concerning whether or not God's intentions were pure and that He was protecting their best interests; satan got man to question whether God wanted to protect them from consuming fruit from the Tree of the Knowledge of Good and Evil or whether God simply did not want them to know as much as He did (Genesis 3:5). When man chose to consume and eat of the Tree of the Knowledge of Good and Evil, he turned his back on childlike acceptance and trust in God and instead pursued his own "wisdom".

In biblical times, when one spoke of knowing someone or something that implied having or acquiring intimate knowledge, not just making a cursory acquaintance. So when man chose to pursue the Knowledge of Good and Evil, satan knew he could then entice man into wanting to experience the full range of Good and Evil. Remember, satan has a counterfeit for every good thing that God has created for man and so satan presented all sorts of choices of enticing-looking things that in reality were not good whatsoever for man. However, man in his pursuit for knowledge and wisdom on his own, bit by bit chose to experience the full range of enticements that satan provided within the world.

Man also made knowledge one of his gods and became consumed with trying to figure everything out and trying to understand everything and in so doing, he set aside his childlike trust and any willingness to simply put his faith in anyone else, let alone God. Pride gripped the heart of man and he became consumed with figuring things out so that he would be the "smartest one in the room", so to speak.

Since satan is a created being and did not have the divine breath of God blown into him as man did when made in the image of God, he has no ability to create original things on his own. satan takes the things of God and counterfeits them by putting his own wicked twist on them. A good example is the feeling people get from taking drugs - it is a counterfeit of the feeling we get in the presence of God. satan knows that if he can derail man through drug use and abuse and then put shame on him for taking drugs, then satan has a chance of keeping man out of the presence of God where there is fullness of joy and freedom in the Spirit. When we make poor choices and we get off track, we are not able to reach our Destiny in Christ until we recalibrate our Kingdom Compass. satan instigates things, irritates and infuriates, and does whatever he can to divert our attention to him and his schemes. His motivation is his unfulfilled desire to be worshipped more than God by us. He manipulates and generates circumstances designed to deceive people into thinking he has the authority that was really returned to man through what Jesus accomplished on the cross; the authority Father God gave man originally and then reiterated immediately after man fell from grace in the Garden. God is all about relationship and His desire from the very beginning has been to have a relationship with man so that He can love us. God created us with the capacity to be carriers of His Glory, to be temples to house the Trinity. He made us to serve as His dwelling place as we invite His son Jesus to live in our hearts and receive the Baptism of the Holy Spirit. We will never know our true identity in Christ until we surrender our lives to Him and grant Him Lordship so all three members of the Godhead can rest, rule, and abide in us. Until we do this, we will never know what it is to be loved or how to love. Our lifetime here on earth is our opportunity to learn to Love God above all else and to learn to Love ourselves as He made us to be so that we can Love our neighbor as we love ourselves.

Jesus Brought The Kingdom to Earth

When Jesus arrived on the scene and began His Ministry, He made it very clear that it is impossible to enter the Kingdom of God without having childlike faith (Hebrews 11:6) and trust in God. Fortunately, God so loved man that He never gave up on him and He provided a way for us to enter in to relationship again with Him (John 3:16). It was very costly for God to purchase us back out of that field of the world where we were stuck, pursuing knowledge for knowledge's sake rather than pursuing following Jesus and the path which He calls us to walk as Christians.

When Jesus completed His assignment on the cross, satan knew all was lost. He knew he no longer had any legitimate authority on Earth or in Heaven. Father God gave authority over ALL things on Earth and in Heaven to

Jesus (Matthew 28:18). The only way satan can accomplish his desires is through stealing our authority by fooling us into accepting his status quo.

Becoming a Born Again Christian

When we are born again, our spirit man is completely reborn and is extremely sensitive to the Spiritual Realm. satan is well aware of this and he also knows that as young baby Christians we are not yet fully confident in our identity in Christ. So what satan will do is, he will cause one of his minions to whisper thoughts near us and when we pick up on those thoughts it is possible for us to be fooled into thinking that they are our own thoughts and the minute we do that, we inadvertently come into agreement with those thoughts and then they do become ours.

The same is true with lying symptoms and sickness. Sometimes we will experience a Spiritual malady and think that it is ours and in doing so we come into agreement with it by taking ownership of it and then it is ours. For instance, when we take a look at the scripture *"If any man be in Christ, he is a new creation, all things are made new"* (2 Corinthians 5:17) there is an incredible promise from Father God! We can use that promise to refuse to receive the Spirit of Infirmity, as well as to refuse to continue to be as we were before we made Jesus Christ the Lord of our lives.

The challenge is that satan knows that we're not yet fully confident and so he will continue to badger us, asking us over and over again "did he really say that?" and "are you sure that what he said is enough?" Are you sure that what Jesus did on the Cross was enough to cover you?" "Are you sure, are you sure?" **Yes, I am sure!** I have no doubt that God is good! I have no doubt that God is the giver of all good gifts (James 1:17) and I have no doubt that what Jesus accomplished on the Cross is good enough for me! I have no doubt that His love never fails (Psalm 136)!

In order to get us off track as we pursue our Christian identity as we learn who we were created to be by reading our Bibles, satan has done whatever he can to twist our concept of sin. In the eyes of Father God, all sin is equal because the wages of sin is Death and all sin leads to Death. All sin is excruciating to God. Remember, He sent His only begotten Son so that no one should perish (John3:16). The one degree twist that satan has managed to slip in to the whole sin debate is that one sin is greater than another. For example, stealing food so that you don't starve to death does not seem to be as bad as murdering a man so that you could steal his wife. But in the eyes of God, actually in the heart of God, ALL sin is excruciating because it prevents His Sons and Daughters from being with Him in Eternity. Yet man has developed a Hierarchy of Sin and then because of our fundamental nature, we point to what other people are doing in an attempt to rationalize what it is that we want to do.

From the moment we step off the straight and narrow path that Father God has called us to, it is a slippery slope! It is interesting to note that from the very beginning in the Garden of Eden when satan kept asking Eve "did he really say that? ...did he really say that? ...did he really say that?" Her response was "Yes He said that and He also said ..." When she responded that way, she played right into satan's hands because she embellished and added to what Father God had said instead of sticking to the straight and narrow truth.

Until we are confident in Who and Whose we are, and know that we are loved no matter what, we will always find ourselves trying to justify our way of seeing the world. We will always try to justify our need to have it our way. In reality though, it's not a "pick and choose" Bible where we get to decide which parts of the Bible we like and want to apply to our lives and which parts are too difficult for us. Rather, the entirety of the Bible is first and foremost God's love letter to us and secondarily our compass for navigating this world. The Bible contains His truth which equates to True North for the Navigator or the one who wants to get somewhere. I don't know about you, but I want to get to the place where I am more of the person that He wants me to be and made me to be, than I am the person who I was stuck being when I was simply reacting to whatever the world slapped me with.

We exalt you Father God.
We sing praises to you.
Let the meditations of our hearts
And the words of our lips be set upon you.
May they arise as a sweet savor to you,
Oh Most High God.
You alone are God over the Universe.
You alone are the bringer of life.
You have breathed your breath of life
Into us and awakened our hearts
To thirst for the More of you, just as
The deer pants for water, every
Cell of our being longs for you, Father God!

Oh Lord Jesus~
You loved us when we were still dead in our ways, still asleep and not yet awakened to your great Love. Thank you for your unending Love - for it never fails! You alone are steadfast and true and now that we are awakened to your great Love, we hunger after you more and more! We want to look upon your face that we may be transformed by Your glory to reflect You more and more, becoming the Light of the world and the Salt of the earth for those who have not met you yet. May we pursue you in unity, in Spirit and in Truth, and may we reflect You well, bringing Life to a dying generation. May we awaken in them the ardent desire to pursue You forever more. May we freely give that which we have freely received from Your Loving hands, and may Your Glory cover the land as the nations realize that You, Lord Jesus, are their true desire!

Come to the Cross of Christ
To see what true Love cost.
Dying before self and man
Is the only way to truly understand!
He loved us first
With a love so very pure
He was willing to endure
All manner of suffering and pain,
All the while counting it gain
So we can arise as His Church.
His body was broken
That we may become His Body,
Holy and Pure,
That those who are steadfast and endure
In his name,
Might be clothed in His Righteousness
As we arise & shine,
Awakening the dawn, for it is time
To declare the Glory of the Lord everywhere!

Holy Spirit,
Where would we be without You? For You truly are the unsung Hero - guiding us in all Revelation and sealing Heavenly Truth in our hearts. You guide our feet, keeping us upon the Narrow Path and making our way straight as we make our way through this fallen world. You grant us access to the Mind of Christ, forever gracing us with heaven's solutions within our daily lives. You bring divine adventure to our lives and help us navigate challenges in

a Christ-like way. You give us words to inspire slumbering
hearts to awaken to the dawning of a new day.

For today is the Day of Salvation!
Today is a new day and Father God
Is doing a new thing, something
Exceedingly and abundantly above
And beyond anything we have ever
Hoped for or imagined!
For today is the Day of His Exaltation
It truly is the Lord's Day forever more!

satan's Plan for Man

The Bible implicitly warns us that satan came to steal, kill
and destroy. It also tells us that he is the father of all lies.
satan has no future. When he comes against us as "the
accuser of the brethren", he is always accusing us about
some way in which we failed in our past. One of the
easiest techniques that I know for disarming his
accusations within our lives is to consider the thought
we're having. If it is negative and about our past, then it is
from the enemy, satan. If it is positive and encouraging
and about our future, then it is from God. Well, the good
thing about knowing a lie is that when you know
something is a lie you can then flip it and flip it good,

knowing that the exact opposite of a lie is the truth and "it is the truth that shall set you free"!

People Can Also Twist Scripture

2 Peter 3:16 tells us, *"…in which are some things hard to understand, which untaught and unstable people twist to their own destruction, as they do also the rest of the Scriptures"* Jesus told his disciples you're either for Him or against Him (Luke 9:50). We cannot afford to be lukewarm, for God will spew us out of His mouth (Revelation 3:16). Wisdom was with Him in the beginning (Proverbs 8:22) when He created the world, therefore ignorance is not of Him. God is steadfast (Psalm 136 and Lamentations 3:22-23). He is unmovable, unshakable in all His ways therefore anything unstable is not of Him. When we realize ignorance and instability are not of God, then they must be from satan. satan is the one who twists scripture; he manipulates and uses it to his own ends. We need to cultivate our ear to hear (Matthew 11:15) what it is we need to know as we seek out True North so that we can calibrate our kingdom compass on True North and then we know we will arrive at our intended destination. We will not be found to be off track or lost, running around on our own and marching to the beat of our own drummer, instead we will know God is leading us straight into the heart of His Destiny and Purpose for us.

One of the things that we need to keep in mind about satan is that since he was designed with the ability to create beautiful worship music as he merely moved across Heaven, he understands the power of music. After all, that ability is what caused him to decide to pursue his own way of doing things by deciding that he should be worshipped instead of God. When he entered into rebellion and fell from Grace, he realize that one of the greatest weapons he had was his ability to use music against mankind. Have you noticed how so much of the music today has an angry beat and a lot of the lyrics are filled with anger and rage? satan is fully aware that man is much more readily able to receive things in his Spirit through music and song than he is through the spoken word. It's very important for us as Christians to monitor what it is that we are taking in to our Spirit man through the gateway of our ears as we hear lyrics that are angry.

We also need to be very careful about what it is we watch. Most of the things that are on television nowadays are "bending their knee" to our culture and are not wholesome or edifying to our Spirit man. Why would we watch something on TV, for instance, an intimate scene between a man and a woman, when we would not stand in their living room and watch? The Bible is very clear that we need to hold every thought captive and present it to Jesus to determine whether or not it's the truth and something that is good for us or whether it is a lie deliberately created to undermine the well-being of our Spirit. We also need to be extremely careful what thoughts we allow ourselves to receive because thoughts eventually become actions. We need to really take all thoughts captive to the obedience of Jesus. The Bible specifically tells us "my people perish for lack of knowledge." I believe that the Church needs to actively begin to teach the Body of Christ strategies for protecting ourselves against the wiles of satan. We need to know strategies that work effectively and what it is that we can do in order to safeguard ourselves from spiritual sabotage by the enemy.

The single greatest deception that satan has pulled off so far is in getting the world to believe that he does not exist. Pretty much anyone you speak to within the world would readily acknowledge that there is such a thing as evil, but when you press them concerning the existence of the devil they suddenly get quiet. I think one of the great problems is in this world is that we tend to subscribe to the theory that "seeing is believing". When we don't see things, we hesitate to believe in them. However, the Bible tells us that *"we wrestle not against flesh and blood but against spiritual entities"* (Ephesians 6:12). We need to change in this regard; we need to realize that satan is alive and that he comes to steal, kill and destroy (John 10:10). That is his only goal. He wants to steal the worship that we have for God. He wants to kill man because he saw how God loving scooped man up from the dust and then blew His own divine breath of life into man whereas Satan was simply created by the spoken word of God. satan fell from Grace and his position within heaven due to pride and Jesus then came to redeem what satan stole from man in the garden when he caused man to doubt the goodness of God. We need to realize that this really is all out Spiritual War. We also need to invest all of our trust and faith in God, knowing that He can do all things *"exceedingly and abundantly above and beyond what we ever could imagine"* (Ephesians 3:20). We need to remember that God loves us, and that His love never fails (Psalm 136)!

The longer satan can fool man into thinking that he doesn't exist, the more opportunities he has to steal our authority from us. After all, how could you possibly reclaim authority from an entity that doesn't exist? Jesus accomplished everything on the cross and He said it is finished, then He ascended to the right hand of the Father and authority was given to him (Matthew 28:18), period. On that day, satan lost any authority whatsoever that he ever had. The only way that he can continue to operate in this world is by continuing to fool us into thinking that he doesn't exist and that we don't have any authority and that God is still mad at us.

God's Plan For Man

The one degree twist that Satan has put upon the brilliance of Father God's plan to reunite us to him through Jesus dying on the Cross for us is that the world tells us that if we make Jesus the Lord of our life, we will miss out on all of the fun. What an incredible lie! If you stop and think about the things that you're no longer supposed to do once you're a follower of Jesus, you will realize after about 3 seconds that each and every one of those things only ever leads to death as well as a whole lot of shame in the process! You may ask "how can you make such a broad statement?" It is easy! I refer you to Romans 6:23 which clearly states that *"the wages of sin is death."* So in reality, all of the things that you're no longer allowed to do once you become a Christian are actually in your best interest to stop doing. Given the choice would you choose death or Eternal life? If you like drinking, picture a drink of whatever your favorite beverage is and then picture Jesus standing right next to it right in front of you. Quick question: What would you reach for? [Note: this technique of picturing Jesus is actually an extremely effective tool for people who are trying to overcome addiction.]

Another technique satan uses is to tell us that Jesus only gave that authority to His direct Disciples, and those gifts are not for us today. That's a lie because the Bible tells us that Jesus is *"the same today that He always ever was and always ever will be"* (Hebrews 13:8). Jesus is the great constant. He is the beginning and the end (Revelation 22:13). And He did what He did and then ascended to heaven in order that His Father would send us the Holy Spirit to comfort us and to guide us as we enforce the victory of the Cross within the world. Jesus knew that we would need guidance. He did what He needed to and then told us He would never leave us, nor forsake us (Hebrews 13:5). That means He's never going to leave us hanging, stuck without help or a ready resource in time of need.

The Bible also tells us that the greatest, and only unpardonable sin is to blaspheme the Holy Spirit (Luke 12:10, Matthew 12:31-32, and Mark 3:28-29). What that means is that when we deny the witness of the Holy Spirit as to what Jesus accomplished on the Cross, not only are we removing any power whatsoever from Christianity today, but we are also blaspheming the Holy Spirit. I believe God wants better for His children. I believe He wants us to have every weapon possible so that we can succeed in our assignment which is to follow Jesus and undo the works of evil that satan has perpetrated upon the world.

False Evidence Appearing Real (FEAR) About satan

In the Garden of Eden, satan - our enemy - was described as a snake and after Adam and Eve allowed him to introduce doubt into their relationship with God, his consequence was that God declared: *"because you have done this, cursed are you above all livestock, and above all Beasts of the field; on your belly you shall go, and dust you shall eat all the days of your life."* (Genesis 3:14)

In the Book of Revelation of Jesus Christ, satan is depicted as a dragon. It seems his appearance has changed in our perception; this is solely because satan is a liar and a thief. On the day Jesus rose from the grave and descended to His rightful position at the right hand of our Heavenly Father, God, Jesus was given *"all authority"* (Matthew 28:18). On that day, satan lost any authority he ever had. The only way he has any authority is by fooling us into giving him power when he actually has none.

The Bible states that satan prowls around "like a lion"; he is not a lion, he only attempts to scare us into believing he has the authority of a lion. The only real lion we need to know about is the Lion of Judah, our Lord and Savior, Jesus Christ. The Bible also informs us that eventually, satan and the other fallen angels get cast into the Lake of Fire to be tormented forever and warns that it is far better for us to do whatever is necessary to go to Heaven rather than taking the risk of going to hell *"where their worm does not die and the fire is not quenched" (Mark 9:44).* The description of satan as a worm reiterates the fact that he is lowly and was cursed by God to forever crawl on his belly with the ever-present reality that the offspring of Eve are empowered to "bruise his head". We need to remember that we were made in the image of our Heavenly Father and we have no reason to ever doubt His perfect Love for us which is more than enough to cast out all fear (**F**alse **E**vidence **A**ppearing **R**eal). For we know that *"His love never fails"* (Psalm 136).

Compasses

Sometimes when we don't know exactly where it is that we are traveling to, the best idea is to use a compass. For example, if you were lost in the woods you would use a compass in order to find your way. However, if your compass is off by even just one single degree, the longer you travel using that compass, the farther off track you will be. If you are traveling using a compass, on the ocean or even by aircraft, and your compass is off by one degree, by the time you have traveled 60 nautical miles you will actually be one nautical mile away from your destination.

The same is true for our Christian walk. If I am walking with the Lord and I am making my decisions based upon skewed truth, the farther I travel following those misconceptions, the farther away from my desired result I will be. The initial intent behind the Separation of Church and State was to ensure that the Government could not require the people to be members of any particular Religion. After all, that is why the Colonists left England…Religious persecution. When we consider the way the Separation of Church and State is misinterpreted today, we can easily see how far off track it is possible to get when our Kingdom Compass is not properly calibrated over a long period of time. This is why it's imperative for us to recalibrate our Kingdom compass. The best way that I can think of to accomplish that is by allowing my mind to be transformed as I renew it (Romans 12:2) by reading what the Bible says truth is and applying those truths to my life as led by the Holy Spirit.

Jesus Chose to Go Low For Us

Jesus girded himself with a towel and then He went low and He began to wash the feet of the disciples with the same towel with which He had girded Himself. He had to go low in order to wash all of the dirt and the filth from the world off of them at their lowest point of contact with the world. He even washed the feet of Judas despite knowing the position of his heart towards Him. Peter tried to refuse Jesus washing his feet, but Jesus informed him that if he did not let Jesus wash his feet, he would have no part of Him (John 13). Jesus also shared the first Communion with them. After they'd been cleansed from worldliness, and had partaken of the Bread of Life and symbolically drunken the Blood of Jesus, they were then able to begin walking out their assignment and their Destiny without Jesus being physically present with them. In reality, all He asks is that we first invite Him in to our own hearts and lives, and that we then be willing to introduce others to the possibility of Him in their lives.

Babes in the Woods

Once we choose to receive the gift of Salvation that Jesus offers us, we need to learn how to navigate our new lives as Christians. At this point, we could easily be considered to be "babes in the woods". The challenge is that since we have only just been removed from the World (John 15:19) by Jesus, our Spiritual Compass has not yet been recalibrated to what our new True North is. True North is actually the pursuit of Kingdom Life which is only found by becoming intimately familiar with how God sees us to be and who it is that He made us to be. True North can only be accurately pursued as we learn as much as we can about the Kingdom of God by making His Holy Bible our new plumb-line, or our new True North. That's why it is so vitally important for us to bring every new thing that we learn about the Kingdom back to God in order to find out what it is He wants us to know. He is the only one who fully knows exactly who it is that He made us to be and what our Divine Purpose is within His Kingdom. For these reasons, God is the only one who can actually completely recalibrate our Kingdom Compass using all sorts of different input. His Holy Bible is first and foremost as our source of understanding of what True North is. Father God will also bring other Kingdom-minded Believers alongside of us to speak into our lives and to pour into us as they disciple us while we get on our feet as Christians. The Holy Spirit is also instrumental in giving us the power and fortitude to walk out our new lives as Christians, boldly demonstrating the difference that His Love is making in our lives! Throughout all of it, Jesus is the one who we pursue! We want to be more and more like Him each and every day so that we know that we know that we know that we are the Bride who ravishes His heart! He deserves nothing less!

The only way that I have discovered to successfully change who it is that I am at a fundamental level is by learning who God says He made me to be and then going after the lies that the world has thrown at me over time. Some of those lies might be: that I have to have someone else in my life in order to be considered successful or worthwhile; that I have to have a house and a yard and a picket fence in order to be considered successful; that I have to have a certain amount of money in my bank account in order to be considered successful. While these are some of the things that the world has placed a priority upon, I don't believe that these are as important to Father God. In fact, Father God tells me that His thoughts about me outnumber the grains of sand on the beach (Psalm 139:18) and the stars in the night sky. I believe that He references the grains of sand on the beach because those are seen readily during the daytime and the stars in the sky are seen at night and therefore I can take comfort knowing that He thinks about me both night and day! He tells me that His thoughts about me are good thoughts, that He rejoices over me with singing (Zephaniah 3:17). Father God is also most certainly not overly concerned about the type of house that I'm living in because the Bible tells me that Jesus Himself said that He has gone to prepare a place for me in His Father's many mansions (John 14:2), therefore my living circumstances for the short time that I am here on earth aren't of the utmost concern or something to worry about. As far as money is concerned, Father God owns the cattle on a thousand hills (Psalm 50:10) and there is no shortage of treasure within His kingdom vaults, in fact, He encourages us to store up our treasure in heaven (Matthew 6:20) and not be concerned with earthly treasure.

One final point to ponder:

if you ever feel as though you don't matter because nobody is else is in your life, Jesus Himself, by doing what He did on the Cross, made you someone worth dying for! So if satan has been trying to beat you up and make you think that you're inconsequential because you don't have someone significant in your life, remember this: satan is the father of all lies (John 8:44), all he ever does is lie. He is incapable of telling the truth, therefore whenever you hear those negative thoughts **flip it and flip it good** and know that the exact opposite of a lie is the Truth, therefore you're not inconsequential - you're some one of great consequence to the kingdom. Jesus gave His own life that you might be with Him in Eternity and Father God truly does delight over you. The Bible tells us that He knew us before the foundation of the world (Ephesians 1:4) and He chose us! *"Now stay focused on Jesus who designed and perfected our faith. He endured the cross and ignored the shame of that day because he focused on the joy that was set before him and now he is seated beside God on the throne, a place of honor."* (Hebrews 12:2)

Kingdom Hopes and Dreams

I hear the Lord inviting us to bring our hopes and dreams to Him. He is the Lord of increase and everything He touches comes to life and is transformed into Life more Abundant! He is the Lord of the harvest and when we partner with Him and choose to plant the seeds He gives us in His field, He will bring increase.

When we share what we have been given with others, He will bless it and multiply it just as the Bible tells us about when Jesus fed the multitude. First He looked around to see what they had been given and then He thanked the Father for what they had and as the Disciples gave the broken bread out, God multiplied it! Jesus Himself handed out the fish which had been broken. After everyone had eaten their fill, the Disciples collected the leftovers; there were twelve baskets worth, one for each Disciple!

There were five loaves of bread which points to the grace of God as He chose to give us His Son, the Bread of Life. There were two fish which points to the importance of our witness to the world as Christians. The twelve baskets point to the Disciples being equipped with Bread of Life with which to feed the broken ones coming into the Kingdom as the Disciples headed out to be Fishers of Men.

I believe Father God had given us all dreams deep within our hearts. The Bible tells us that He will grant the desires of their hearts to those who take their delight in him, and that *"no eye has seen, nor ear heard, nor the heart of man imagined what it is that God has prepared for those who love Him"* (1Corinthians 2:9) I believe that when we choose to take those dreams which may still just be seeds, and partner with God, He will bring the increase. Our dreams will be amazing as we be partner with Father God and they come forth, greatly advancing His kingdom!

Offer Up a Sacrifice of Praise

Are you being given a chance to sing the sacrifice of praise in the middle of dying to self and laying your life down for Jesus and others? Count it all joy. The Bible instructs us and even commands us to count it all joy, just as Jesus endured the Cross for the joy set before Him. What if He knew how filled with joy His Father would be when He, the Son of Man chose to worship as He drank His cup... A bitter cup of humiliation, accusation, and the darkest of evil, human suffering? Not my will, but yours Father - because I know you, I trust you and your love for me implicitly - no doubt - no hesitation - no reservation - no second-guessing - I know you and burn as one with your heart for your children so I lay my life down as a sacrifice of praise to you - the one I have always been with - the one who chose me first - the Creator of the Universe - the Ancient of Days.

God's Forgiveness

If I stopped to think
On all the reasons
I should be disqualified
From receiving your Love,
I'd be overwhelmed
With such grief and remorse
Welling up deep from within
That I would surely miss the point:

There's no thing I could ever do,
No life I could manage to live,
That would ever come close
To being justified
Or even worthy of earning that great gift
Which you offer so freely,
Simply due to grace
And the nature of your Love.

You alone are forgiveness.
Your Love washes over me,
Setting me free to be forever yours,
Forever open to renewing my Spirit.
When I focus on you,
Circumstances melt away
And Hope wells up, pushing doubt aside
For you are forever magnified.
Larger than life is your Love.
You alone ignite my heart, consuming me
Until together we are one in eternity.

Eternal Hope in Christ

Jesus Pursues

The Father's heart is blessed
When Faith has shown her light
In the midst of worst circumstance.

Judgment is forced to bow
When heaven's mercy is stressed
In spite of evil's intent.

Hearts rejoice with newfound Hope
As spirits come alive
Right in the here and now.

Oh Jesus, how you change the world!
Awakening dreams deep within:
Stored up treasures with no expiration date,
Future solutions – never too late,
Game changers,
Only released through Heaven's gate.

Lord Jesus, you are never too late!
Offering us all a chance to participate,
As Heaven turns the world upside down
... One heart at a time!

Eternal Hope in Christ
June 11, 2018

New Life in Jesus

My heart sings by your Spirit,
Bubbling up with joy
Until others can hear it.
You are the Creator who dreamed it,
The very Word which was spoken,
And you continue to hold ALL things together
Despite what man has broken.

All of Heaven KNOWS Your Name!!!

You breathed us into being,
Part of Your great Plan
To reveal the Wisdom of your ways,
Using what was once foolish in deed
To reach out now to others still in need.

Peace Maker ~ Sin Breaker

You are LOVE in action.
Forgiving us all our wrongs.
At our weakest you come along,
Making us strong.
Breaking sin's hold -
Those dark patterns of old.
You alone set us FREE,
Rewriting our apparent story
To bring Your Father ALL the Glory!

Eternal Hope in Christ

Chapter 2: Changing to Kingdom Perspective

Lenses of the World

From the moment we enter our lives on Earth, we begin accumulating experiences which determine the way we assimilate and understand future experiences. In short, our experiences provide us a lens through which we look at the world. The problem is that if our lenses are significantly impacted by negative and adverse events, it can cause us to pull away from others and to misinterpret their actions.

In reality, most people are simply trying to get through the day; they are just trying to survive. Most people do not wake up wondering what they can do to hurt us on a given day. We need to work on recalibrating the way we see the world and understand that the world doesn't revolve around us and our experiences. As we pursue wholeness and heart healing, we are offered a chance to bit by bit remove the lies which we have been believing or which have been bombarding us; the lies which have been telling us that we are useless, worthless, unlovable, ignored, rejected, and all sorts of other less than desirable qualities.

The only way that we can really renew the way we see the world is by allowing our minds to be transformed (Romans 12:12) as we apply God's Truth as our moral compass as well as our plumb-line. Our plumb-line is the standard by which we interact with the world. When we do this, bit by bit the lies fall away and bit by bit we become whole as we realize that in a lot of instances our sadness is triggered by us over-interpreting other people's actions as being responses to us, rather than understanding their actions as simply being their way of surviving and navigating this world.

Covenant Declaration

Lord,

I am inclining my ear to you.
As I come to you, I am listening to you that my soul may live and prosper.

Lord,

You have made an Everlasting Covenant with me.
Be my defender.

Lord,

I seek your heart more and more each day.
I am seeking you in the midst of this.

I am calling upon you as you are near,
For you will never leave me nor forsake me.
Lord,

I confess that my thoughts are not yet your thoughts,
And my ways are not yet your ways,
For as the heavens are higher than Earth,
So too are your ways much higher than mine.
And your thoughts are higher as well.

Lord,

Help me to see through the lens of your Covenant with me.

Help me to know your steadfast love will not depart from me,
And that your Covenant of Peace shall not be removed.

Thank you Lord for going before me to prepare my way,
And for always being with me.

Thank you that you are my Fortress,
In you I am safe and loved.

Thank you for the blood of your son,
Jesus Christ, My Lord and Savior!

I plead the blood of Jesus over my life,
And I thank you, Lord Jesus, for setting me free!
It is in your Holy, precious name that I pray, Lord Jesus,
Amen.

Eternal Hope in Christ

The Truth About Forgiveness

In our lives there are consequences for the choices that we make. Unfortunately, sometimes we don't realize the fullness of those consequences within the Spiritual Realm. A good example of this is when we choose to not forgive others for the things that they have done to us, whether or not they knew what they were doing.

When we partner with the Spirit of Unforgiveness or the Spirit of Offense, we cripple ourselves spiritually. In essence, it would be like drinking a cup of rat poison and hoping the other guy dies. That's just not the way it works! The unfortunate reality is that in the majority of instances, the person who has hurt us doesn't even realize the fullness of what we experienced in the exchange. As we relive that moment of hurt over and over and over again in our heads, we are allowing that person to have way more power over us than we would ever choose to do if we thought about it logically and without emotion.

Seriously, if what they did was bad enough to require forgiveness from us, then why choose to relive that moment day after day after day? If our current opinion of that person is actually correct, why choose to give that person the power to destroy more of our time living our lives here on earth? In short, why continue to rent space in our heads to that person? Or why choose to give them the power to ruin another moment of our life?

The truth is that forgiveness is a choice. It's a choice we make for ourselves! We are choosing to no longer live our lives tied to the offender who has hurt us. We are choosing to no longer allow that person to hurt us again, day after day after day. As we choose to forgive, we are not saying that what they did was alright with us. Instead, we are choosing to step into a healthier Spiritual condition. We are choosing to give that person to the Lord in order that they might no longer take away from our current Spiritual wholeness. Ideally, as we choose to forgive, we choose to trust the Lord that He has a better plan. We are choosing to trust that He turns all things together for the good of those who love Him and are called according to His purposes (Romans 8:28). We are choosing to invest in His Kingdom when we release forgiveness to another person on earth because they will then have forgiveness released to them in Heaven (Matthew 18:18)! What if what they really needed was a Spiritual upgrade and because they were bound to us through unforgiveness, they were temporarily blocked from moving onward in the Kingdom?

The Bible gives us many examples of the toxic effects of unforgiveness within the parables Jesus shared with His disciples throughout the Gospels. The Parable of the Unforgiving Servant is pretty clear about the Father's heart concerning forgiveness:

A servant owed a debt he could never pay and was forgiven the debt only to then go and demand payment from others. The master confronted the servant and chastised the wicked servant. *"His master was angry, and delivered him to the torturers until he should pay all that was due him* (remember this was a 'debt he could never pay'!)." Jesus continued on to warn us that *"so my Heavenly Father also will do to you if each of you, from his heart, does not forgive his brother his trespasses."*

Basically, Jesus is warning us that since we have been forgiven a debt we could never repay, we need to forgive our brothers (and sisters) of anything they may have done to us, otherwise we will find ourselves placed in prison (Spiritually) and given over to the torturers until we repay our (unpayable) debt. Unforgiveness halts our Spiritual progress and actually even opens us up to legal harassment/torture by satan. Jesus also warned His disciples that *"it is impossible that no offenses should come, but woe to him through whom they do come!"* (Luke 17:1)

Choose wisely!

The Truth About Judgments

In order to be a judge, one has to be thoroughly familiar with the topic they are passing judgment on. You must be a resident expert on the thing you are judging. We need to stop and think about what our judgments say about us. The Bible warns us that we shall be measured by the same standard by which we judge others (Matthew 7:2).

Think before you speak and look before you leap. Measure twice, cut once. The first cut is the deepest – whom have we cut deeply, unnecessarily?

The Bible also tells us to not judge anyone until we have walked in their shoes. How can we begin to understand someone else until we have taken time to know them and learn about their life circumstances? Jesus came down to walk on earth so we would know that He understood our difficulties and challenges and still prevailed, overcoming the world as well as sin and death!

Our judgments, based upon outward appearances, have caused many to walk out of the church which is supposed to be the Lord's House. Jesus is the gate, not us. He alone knows their hearts (Jeremiah 17:10). He lived our lives while on the cross (He experienced our sins and the whole portion of our lives before we knew Him, along with our lives after we invited Him to live inside of us) yet He chose to forgive ALL of us (Luke 23:34)! He invites ALL inside to encounter His heart and experience His great Love.

We were never meant to judge who could come in and who would be refused entrance to His Kingdom. There is no one whose heart He does not want to touch with His great Love. We need to look to our own hearts and see what judgments we need to set aside.

There truly are people who have never heard of the Love Jesus has for them. How will they know if we are unwilling to approach them as his ministers of reconciliation (2 Corinthians 5:11-21)?

Jesus warns us in Luke Chapter 19 that "the spirit of offense will come, however, woe to the one who brings it." This truth reminds us how important it is for us to not risk getting offended by aligning ourselves with the Spirit of Offense when we try to interpret what is happening in the world around us. The best thing that we can do is to use Jesus as our lens and try to learn how to see the world through his eyes, always consulting the Holy Spirit to learn "what does this mean?" and "what must I do?"

Our Circumstances

In general, our circumstances separate out into three categories that I've noticed. The first category would be circumstances that are actually the consequence of a less-than-ideal choice on our part. The second set of circumstances would be an opportunity for us to develop a greater level of Integrity within our moral character. The third set of circumstances would be an opportunity for us to allow the Lord to lead us through what would seem to be a valley in our lives. In this instance, it is only when we allow the Lord to bring us out of our circumstances that we then gain a whole new level of authority over that particular issue within our lives. Remember, the Bible tells us that *"they overcame by the blood of the Lamb, the word of their testimony, and not loving their old life unto death"* (Revelation 12:11). I believe that this means that what Jesus accomplished for me on the cross and His presence in my life together have led me to the point where I no longer want to hold on to my old way of living life. When I let go of my old way of living my life and give it to Him, He will bring me through. When I then share the Testimony of what Jesus did for me, it gives the next person hope AND Jesus is able to redeem my history while at the same time leading another person through their valley of difficulty. What an awesome God we serve!

Did you ever take a moment to consider why the enemy only ever accuses us about events in our past? One reason is that he has no future and therefore does not operate in terms of the future. Another reason is that he knows that we have no ability to change our past on our own. However, when we give our lives to Jesus, He can! He can take the worst thing we feel we ever walked through and turn it into a victory! The Bible even tells us that He *"turns all things together for the good of those who love Him and are called according to His purposes"* (Romans 8:28). Once again, our challenge is a matter of perspective. It is as if Father God is working on a tapestry from "up" in Heaven, and we are down here on Earth, looking at the back side of it, trying to make some sort of sense of it. The good news is that the closer we grow to the Lord, the easier it can be for us to have confidence in Him and the record of His nature (which is to bless His Sons and Daughters!)

I believe that most of the circumstances that we find ourselves in offer us the opportunity to increase our trust in God. I believe He is always reaching out to us, asking us "do your trust me on this?" The Bible tells us that He turns all things together for the good of those who love Him and are called according to His purposes (Romans 8:28). The Bible also tells us that He *"chose us out of the world before the foundation of the world"* (Ephesians 1:4). That's amazing! I believe that God is always wanting to increase our faith. The Bible tells us that Jesus is the *"author and perfecter of our faith"* (Hebrews 12:1-3). So I believe that we are continuously being afforded opportunities to choose to trust God and invest our faith in Him and when we do, we receive Kingdom rewards. Anytime we invest our faith in the Kingdom there is an amazing Harvest to be yielded, treasure in heaven (Matthew 6:20) as it were! God is the god of increase (1 Corinthians 3:7) and as we choose to place our faith in Him, He is a rewarder of that faith. Remember, it says that it is impossible to please God without faith (Hebrews 11:6). Every time we place our faith in God, we please him. What an awesome thing, to be able to please the Creator of the Universe, the one True Living God!

The way that we believe ourselves to be deep within our hearts determines the goals that we set as well as our behavior on a daily basis. The good news (Gospel) is that we can *"be transformed by the renewing of our minds"* (Romans 12:12). God can easily help us break free from our old mindset, that stronghold which prevents us from becoming all that we can be in Him. When we read the word (Holy Bible) and take in "the Bread of Life", we gain Spiritual insight into who God made us to be, after all we are *"made In His Image and likeness"* (Genesis 1:26). When we learn who we are as He sees us to be, we get the Revelation that *"we can do all things through Christ Jesus who strengthens us"* (Philippians 4:13). As we grow in Christ and learn who the Lord has called us to be, we may still fall short sometimes of capturing how He sees us. After all, He knows everything and each good gift that He has placed within us as well as what is required to draw it out of us. Our ways are not His ways (Isaiah 55:8) yet, however all things are possible with God (Matthew 19:26) in our lives!

I think sometimes as Christians we tend to give the enemy too much credit. For example, we tend to always put off our current uncomfortable situation to being "attacked by the enemy". Sometimes what we are going through could actually instead be an opportunity for us to develop a greater level of integrity by following the Godly approach to walking with the Lord straight out from the midst of your circumstances. Or it could be the opportunity to step into a whole new level of authority within God's Kingdom by allowing Him to deliver us and in the process acquiring a Testimony of His Grace which can then be used to set another who is struggling free.

We need to remember that yes, as we shift from level to level within the Kingdom of God, satan will test the depth of our confidence in our identity, but God will never allow for us to be sifted by satan or tempted without providing a way out for us (1 Corinthians 10:13). That is where knowing the Bible and mining it for Spiritual Warheads which you can launch right at satan's lies is imperative! The Bible tells us that no weapon formed against can prosper (Isaiah 54:17), however, there will be weapons formed I believe!

What you focus on is what you empower. Have you ever noticed that the more you try to stop a bad habit, the more you find yourself thinking about wanting to do what it is you're trying not to do? For example, if you want to lose weight and stop eating sweets, the harder you try to avoid eating them the more you feel drawn to them. Or if you're trying to quit smoking cigarettes, the more you think about not smoking a cigarette, the more you feel you simply must have one. The basic fact is that whatever we focus on is what we give power to. The best solution to this issue is to focus on Jesus and give Him the power in our lives to help us overcome what it is that we need to set aside in order to be able to pursue Him more effectively. We need to stop focusing on sin and instead receive what it is Jesus accomplished for us on the Cross. He overcame sin and Death on the Cross and because of that, we walk in Victory when we follow Him. The Bible promises that we will be transformed from Glory to Glory (2 Corinthians 3:18). Did you notice that we start at Glory? How awesome is that?!

Breakthrough Declaration

I am confident and I have faith that I will experience the goodness of the Lord in the land of the living!

The Lord has called me and He has chosen to lavish His blessings over all areas of my life. His hand is upon my life and I walk in His favor as I go where He leads me. He is expanding my territory as a testimony to His exceeding greatness!

Because of His unsurpassable goodness --

I will thrive, not merely survive!

I hold on to His promises, resting in His peace beyond all understanding!

I am filled with joyous hope, no matter my apparent circumstance!

I am bold and determined and my faith grows stronger each and every day!

I will not let go of his Words and Promises to me until I experience them!

I will prevail with the spirit of generosity in all areas of my life, attitude and behavior!

I have been blessed beyond measure that I might be a blessing to others, and

I choose to share generously what I have been given with others, expanding his kingdom Wherever I Go!!!

Hallelujah!

Eternal Hope in Christ

The Promise of the Lord

From early on I can remember knowing things ahead of time. There was one time when I was about 12 years old and I was over in Holland to attend a riding camp. Since it was the first time I had been so far away from home, I was extremely homesick. My Oma (the Dutch word for grandmother), thought that the best thing she could do for me would be to take me over to where the camp was going to be each day leading up to the Camp. She would take me over there in the morning and I would spend the day with the people who ran the camp and I would do things ranging from cleaning out horse stalls to serving people coffee in the cafe. On the particular day in question, I was sitting with the young couple that ran the camp and they had a two-year-old son who was playing near his wading pool in front of us. All of the sudden in my mind's eye, I saw him get into the electric vehicle next to the pool and turn the key and I saw the vehicle heading straight at us. Because of this Word of Warning from the Lord, I was able to point out to the parents what he was about to do as he began to do it and they were able to turn the car off and rescue their son as well. So I learned early on to listen to whatever Word of Warning I got, whether it was a voice speaking to me in my head or a sudden thought or a flash of an impression showing me a picture of what was to come. I learned that it was far better to speak up and warn people and have it turn out that nothing happened then it was to not speak up and have something bad that I knew was going to happen, occur.

Even when I was not walking with God and was actually doing things that are generally frowned upon by the rest of good Society, He was always there for me and He was always protecting me and trying to keep me safe. One of the most outstanding examples of this was when I was living in Florida and a friend had asked me to give him a ride over to find out whether he could rent a room from another friend of his. When we got to the other friend's house, I noticed several large dogs at different points on the property. They were not friendly-looking dogs. I was invited into the house, but politely declined, saying that I wanted to smoke a cigarette outside while I waited. (Are you kidding me? I'm not going to enter a house where I have to walk past two vicious dogs to get in because, who knows if they'll let me leave? Seriously!)

After waiting outside for about fifteen minutes, I was joined by the friend whom I had given a ride to and his friend who actually lived at the house. They asked me if I wanted to smoke some pot with them and I said sure. No sooner had we started smoking then the guy who lived there lost his balance and kind of started to fall into the fire pit and I thought "this is not going well". Right after that a car pulled into the driveway and a guy got out and started walking across the lawn towards us. The very second that I saw him in the same frame of view with his brother who owned the house, I very clearly heard a voice say: "You need to get out of here. Somebody is going to get shot!"

You have never seen somebody react so quickly! I looked down at my watch and said "Oh wait, what day is today? Oh my gosh, it's Tuesday?! I'm supposed to be volunteering at my kids' school! I have to go! Hey, can you give him a ride? Awesome! Thanks!" And with that I was off like a shot myself! I didn't think much of it. I just knew that I did what I needed to do. Well, about three months later at 3:00 in the morning, I got a phone call from the guy whom I had given the ride to telling me that the younger brother had just shot and killed his older brother! What a tragedy!

I can't explain why God would care so much about me that He would warn me, all I know is He is that good and His Grace is far greater than we could ever imagine. So I guess my wish is that we would start learning how to grow in Grace ourselves (2 Peter 3:18). And that we would start to work to cultivate a better understanding of how He sees others so that we could treat other people with compassion, kindness and caring (Galatians 5:22-23). I wish that we could learn how to love them no matter how it is they appear to us, knowing that we don't need to understand them to love them. We don't even need to approve of them to love them. It's okay to love someone who is in a homosexual relationship. It's okay to love someone who is addicted to street drugs. It's okay to love someone who is just lost. That's what Jesus did - He Loved us until we could no longer resist Him! He's just that good!

The Pharisee Spirit

It is also dangerous to bend our knee to the pursuit of Knowledge for knowledge's sake. Our culture has made a god out of having to understand every single thing ad infinitum. We have bowed our knee to Knowledge just like the Pharisees did when they pursued knowledge for knowledge's sake and walked away from Spiritual Truth, refusing to even recognize the Son of God when they saw Him face to face. The biggest problem with having to understand everything is that it obliterates childlike faith and trust (Matthew 8:13) and without faith it is impossible to please God (Hebrews 11:6). We need to cultivate our ear to hear (Matthew 11:15) what He has to say to us so that in all instances we can ask Him, "Lord what do you want me to know in this?"

Kingdom Repentance

When Jesus began His ministry, He was often heard saying to people: *"Repent for the kingdom of God is at hand."* (Matthew 3:2) What He meant was: turn from the way in which you are used to considering the world and allow yourself to be opened up to see the way in which God considers things. In this regard, repentance was never meant to be a moment of misery, rather it was meant to be an invitation to receive the fullness of what God has for each and every one of us for the Kingdom of God is made of amazing things and the fruit of the Spirit is kindness, caring, love, compassion, and self-control - all good qualities (Galatians 5:22-23).

People seem to get caught up in the notion of continuously repenting when I believe Father God's intention was for people to grab the moment that was being offered through the Gift of Jesus in order to be truly changed in such a significant way that they would no longer choose to sin; that man would choose to allow the kingdom to invade his very heart, taking residence there and bringing forth the fruit of the Spirit. I believe the idea of "Repent for the kingdom of God is at hand" is the best invitation in the world for it affords us the opportunity to become who it is that God created us to be. When we become that person, we are then able to step right into the center of His Divine Will for our lives and we're able to walk in His ways as we fulfill His purpose through our lives. So I rejoice that because of Jesus I was able to repent, changing the way I consider things in order that I might set my sights on Jesus and follow Him as I am transformed from Glory to Glory!

We need to change the way we think…to renew our minds by coming into agreement with the Kingdom way of seeing things (Romans 12:2). One example of this would be to focus on what God is doing, rather than our worldly circumstances. The world will never show us the Love that Father God showed when He willingly gave His only Son to be the sacrifice to pay for and atone for Man's sin (John 3:16). Because we live in a fallen world and man has made knowledge his god, we seem to always be actively looking for proof that the way that we believe the world to be is correct. In other words, we tend to really stretch to grab ahold of whatever proof we can have that we have figured things out correctly. So, if we tend to see what we seek to see, what if we were always looking for the Kingdom of God to be made manifest? I venture to guess that we would start seeing "proof" of God at work, advancing His Kingdom, all around us. I bet we would even find ourselves having Divine Appointments every single day! Go God!

Inviting the Trinity into Your Life

Heavenly Father, You know my heart. I want to know that you are real. I ask that You reveal Yourself to me that I may experience the love that You have for me.

Lord Jesus, I ask that You would lift my head and call me friend. I want to encounter Your great love for me. I want to be made whole that I may walk by Your side, yoked to You. Bear my burdens and give me rest.

Holy Spirit, Prepare my heart that I may receive the Love of the Father and of my Lord, Jesus Christ, and enter into a relationship with my Heavenly Father through His Son, Jesus.

I want life more abundant. I want to walk in Love as I experience the power of the Gospel in my life and become a living Testimony to the Grace and forgiveness and Love of the Holy Trinity, in Jesus' mighty Name I pray, Amen.

Jesus is Our Advocate

We know that Jesus is in Heaven advocating on our behalf - another way of looking at this is, Jesus is interceding on our behalf on His throne in Heaven (Romans 8:34) that we would succeed in undoing the works of the enemy! Well, we know that the *"Joy of the Lord is our strength"* (Nehemiah 8:10) and we know that Father God *"grants the desires of their hearts to those who take their delight in Him"* (Psalm 37:4). We also know that Jesus always looked to the Father and took His delight in Him while walking the Earth as a man. We also know that Jesus *"endured the Cross for the joy set before*

Him" (Hebrews 12:2) and that was the joy of us being given the opportunity to enter back into right relationship with His Father through what He accomplished for us on the Cross. We know that Jesus descended into Hell, took the keys of Death and Hell away from satan and then ascended to Heaven to sit at the right hand of the Father where He is interceding on our behalf. As Father God hears Jesus's prayers on our behalf, He will surely grant them, and answered prayer brings "fullness of joy", therefore the joy that Jesus will experience as His prayers are answered becomes our strength.

Keep in mind that Jesus actively warned Peter that satan had asked to sift him and He told him that He'd be praying for him and his success (Luke 22:31). As we step into each new level of authority within the Kingdom, the enemy will question whether or not we are really qualified to be there. Remember also that the Bible tells us that His word is *"a lamp unto our feet"* (Psalm 119:105) and that means that whenever we experience a dark time in our lives, if we look to the Bible, His Holy Word, we will see the way in which we should go. Jesus Himself tells us *"He will never leave us, nor forsake us"* (Hebrews 13:5) so we know that He is always with us and because we have access to the mind of Christ, we have access to solutions that the rest of humanity does not yet have. We are to become solutions to our brothers and sisters who are still lost as we point them to Jesus, giving them hope no matter how lost they are.

Declaration of Faith

I am confident and I have faith that I will experience the goodness of the Lord in the land of the living! The Lord has stored up goodness and He is ready to lavish His blessings over all areas of my life that I might be a carrier of His Glory. The Lord will bless me and expand my territory as a testimony to His exceeding greatness! His hand and favor will be evident in my life!

Because of His immeasurable goodness --

I will thrive and not strive!

I will persevere in the promises of God with Joy, Hope and Peace!

I have faith and will not let go of God's promises until I see them come to pass!

I will prevail with a spirit of generosity in my attitude, conduct and giving!

I have been blessed to be a blessing and I will share what I have been given ...freely!

I am strong, determined, courageous and Full of Faith!

I choose to share generously with others, expanding His Kingdom wherever He calls me to go.

Lord, I thank you that even in the wilderness there is the joy of your presence when we choose to ascend to your heart in worship. Thank you for the harvest which is present even in the great valleys of our existence. Give us your heart to see each circumstance as you do that we might reap a harvest wherever we go with you leading us Holy Spirit. May we reflect your Son, Jesus, as we shine brightly in the dark, drawing others to your amazing grace. Amen

Eternal Hope in Christ

Eternal Kingdom Friendships

One of the greatest things about coming back into alignment and walking with the Lord has been learning that all these new friendships that I have made since then are Eternal friendships. Never again will I be without friends! I've also noticed that over the course of my life, whenever something significant was about to happen that would throw me for a loop, God always brought someone alongside me to encourage me and to speak truth to me so that when the enemy tried to undermine my confidence, I was always protected by God's love.

Over the years, many different people have said to me that they just don't understand me, or that there is no one else is quite like me. Well, I guess that could be a compliment. Sometimes it simply made me feel that people didn't really know how to classify me. I don't believe that as Sons and Daughters of the Utmost High God it's our job to classify people or to categorize them. We need to stop trying to freeze frame people by trying to understand them based upon how we see them in one single moment, and instead embrace who it is that they are in Christ, knowing that they are a continuously evolving person. In addition to this, we don't necessarily need to understand someone, rather we need to learn how to love them right where they're at. We need to learn how to encourage them to become the best person that God has made them to be. We need to learn how to honor others. And most of all, we need to learn that it's not about us and how we see someone, rather is ALL about what God wants to bring forth in any given moment.

Strength in Numbers

The simple truth is that man was not made to be alone. Father God realized this after He had made Adam and He then made Eve in order to be the "help meet" for Adam. The Bible tells us that two are better than one because if one should get weary or fall down, the other one can pull them up (Ecclesiastes 4:9-12). Well, I believe that 3 are even better than 2 because then you have a three-strand cord which is not easily broken (Ecclesiastes 4:12). When Father God is in your life and Jesus is the Gateway through which you entered back into right relationship with Father God, and you then add the Holy Spirit as the Comforter, that's the best of all possible situations!

One reason why man should not be alone is because that is when the enemy will come and attack our thoughts and try to undermine our thoughts concerning God. The Bible tells us to *"not lean on our own understanding"* (Proverbs 3:5), but rather, to pursue wisdom by choosing the council of other godly people within our lives. When we include God in our lives, and we cultivate a personal relationship with all three members of the Trinity, that is when we are in the best position to pursue wisdom. When we yoke our mind to the mind of Christ, we have all of the wisdom of the Godhead available to us. The Bible also tells us that wisdom is *"far greater of a treasure than rubies, silver or gold"* (Proverbs 8:11) and that *"fear of the Lord is the beginning of Wisdom"* (Proverbs 9:10). What this means is that when we consider the fullness of God, we should actually be filled with a reverential fear, a complete and utter awe of the Lord!

Kingdom Minded

As Christians, we need to realize that it's no longer about us on any level. When we experience pain, whether it's physical or emotional, we need to realize that it's not about us and how we "feel". Rather, it's an opportunity for us to choose to invest in God's Kingdom and pray for someone else who is being afflicted by that Spirit or by that particular pain. We need to change the way we think and we need to realize that it was never about how we felt about anything. I'm serious. If it was about how man felt about anything, don't you think that God would have answered Jesus's prayer in the Garden of Gethsemane when Jesus said *"if there's any way, let this cup pass from me"* (Matthew 26:39)? God didn't want to turn His back on His Son. God simply knew what the entire picture was and how important what Jesus was going to go through was. God looks at the full picture, whereas we only seem to see the part that affect us directly.

On the Mount of Transfiguration when the Heavens opened, Father God declared *"This in my Son in whom I am well pleased. Hear Him."* (Matthew 17) At that point we were directed by God to hear what Jesus has to say, and Jesus commanded us numerous times to "Follow Me." In the Garden of Gethsemane, Jesus stressed the importance of us (His disciples) seeing what it is He wants us to see in each situation. First He asked them to pray, yet when He returned they were sleeping. He commented on their slumber and then went off again after asking them to watch for awhile. Remember, Jesus only did what He saw His Father doing. I believe that Jesus wanted us to grab ahold of the concept that when we look to what the Father is doing and see Him giving us a cup that we feel is too difficult for us to drink, we need to pray and declare our trust in Him. We need to get to that place where we can honestly and whole heartedly say "Not my will but Your will - I trust You."

Pray Unceasingly

As Christians, instead of praying for someone else to be saved from their moment of discomfort, instead we should be praying "Lord may they receive everything that You have for them within it and may they learn what they need to know so they can move on to the next level of encounter with You, Lord, in Jesus Name. Amen." We need to up our game by refusing to consider or get bogged down with how we "feel" about things and rather instead look to the whole picture of what it is that God is trying to do through whatever the circumstance is. Maybe He's inviting us to pray for someone else. Maybe He's giving us a Word of Knowledge because He wants to heal someone and reveal His Love to them and He knows that we love partnering with Him in order that His Kingdom would expand. We need to get to that point where we trust God so implicitly that we never even hesitate to say: *"Not my will, Lord, but yours"* (Luke 22:42). We need to know that we know that we know that He is good ALL the time and that we trust His Plan because we believe Him when He tells us that He has a Plan to prosper us, giving us Hope of a future with Him (Jeremiah 29:11). Most of all, we need to get our eyes off ourselves and instead look to Jesus, because He is the *"author and finisher of our faith"* (Hebrews 12:2) and He is the one who knows what we need when we need it.

You may have already heard this, but the definition of insanity is: doing the same thing over and over and over again while expecting a different result. I had a friend at one point who would always ask others what was going on in their lives. She had a genuine interest and deeply cared about how others were doing. The problem was that there were some people who would call and just go on and on and on about all the drama going on in their lives and the net result was that my friend became totally worn out by the stress of other people's lives. Especially since they never seemed to want to act on the good advice that she gave them.

Having witnessed this on several occasions when I was visiting her, I felt led to share some of my newly acquired wisdom with her. "The next time they call, the minute they start their litany of complaining, you need to immediately begin to pray with them, thanking God because He has the solution for them, in Jesus' Name. One of two things will happen - they will either get their answer from the Lord which would be the best case ever, or they will stop calling you and you won't end up feeling worn out by all these dramatic phone calls." She agreed that that was really a great approach, however, she never acted on it for whatever reason. Well, a few weeks later I was over and the same thing happened with the same person calling and I reminded her of the advice that I had given her and she agreed once again that it was great advice. Yet she never acted on it that time either.

(Oh the irony of it all! Can you hear Heaven laughing?)

I finally decided to ask God "What is going on here?" He showed me that she had a need to be needed, as we all do deep down inside. I then realized that in an instance where someone seems unable to act upon Godly wisdom, instead of getting frustrated, I need to grab the opportunity to cultivate Grace. I need to realize that I definitely don't want to be responsible for causing that person additional setbacks. What I mean by this is: each time we receive Godly advice yet fail to act upon it, we are held accountable. So as soon as I become aware that the person I'm interacting with has for whatever reason an inability to act on whatever Godly advice has been offered, I need to step away from the situation and disengage and refuse to become a pawn in one of satan's schemes to further derail them. In short, I need to prefer others above myself - I need to respect and honor that person right where they are at and forego my need to "shine brightly as their solution." At the same time that I step away, I also need to actively pray (in tongues) for my friend that they would receive what it is that God wants them to receive in those moments. I need to pray as a blessing for them, rather than as their "solution".

We need to understand that at a fundamental level, each and every person has a deep, deep need to feel needed. Nobody wants to think they could just disappear and no one would notice. However, we need to balance things and we need to realize that the really the most important gift we could ever give anyone is actually pointing them to the Lord as their solution. We do not want to risk inadvertently encouraging others to murmur and complain

114

o us just because we have a need to be needed. Rather, we should always be actively pointing others to Father God, Lord Jesus, and the Holy Spirit in order that they could cultivate an active, ever-increasing depth of relationship with all three members of the Godhead. That should be our goal!

One of the things that I heard somebody say at an AA Meeting once was that "nobody can take our self-respect away." What ends up happening is we make compromises in our life, and each time we do, we give a bit of ourselves away. Bit by bit by bit we can give our self-respect away through the poor choices that we make. I, myself, finally got to a point where I really did not want to look myself in the mirror because I was so filled with shame over my bad choices and the compromises that I had allowed myself to make in the pursuit of friends and what I thought was love. At that point in time I mistook physical intimacy for love because I would not have ever been intimate with anyone I did not have deep feelings for. The problem was that that is not God's Best for anyone - He designed physical intimacy as a part of the intimate, lifelong marriage covenant between one man and one woman.

Anytime we try to take a shortcut, we run the risk of ending up way off track Spiritually. There's a saying that comes to mind: he who cuts corners, goes in circles. So I believe that when we start to make moral compromises, we send ourselves spinning down the wrong track. When we compromise ourselves Spiritually, we are definitely not

115

on the path that God has laid out for our lives - that much is clear.

Jesus Will Never Leave Us

"Fear Not...I Am with you...Even to the end of the age" (Matthew 28:20).

It is the end of the church age where we tried to contain His presence within the walls of a building or limit Him to a particular denomination. The Kingdom arrived with Jesus and He said: *"Repent! Change the way you think and act, for the Kingdom of God is at hand"* (Matthew 3:2). Jesus brought Heaven's way of looking at things down to earth. He challenges us to learn a new way – the way that leads to life.

All of Earth eagerly awaits the unveiling of the Sons of God (Romans 8:19)...Learn to think like Jesus...Stand up and be noticed for how Jesus has changed your thoughts and behavior.

On the Cross, Jesus tore the veil separating man from God (Matthew 27:51). He destroyed the power of sin over man. He is the gate (John 10:9) through which we may choose to enter in to the very heart of the Father, where we can learn true worship in His very presence. Not just singing a song, but truly considering ALL that He has done for us by opening a way for us to seek out the

Father and to be seen by Him as Sons and Daughters. Jesus gets glory as His Father sees how His Son's presence in our hearts and lives has changed us.

As Jesus ministered to people, the Kingdom of God was released and people were profoundly affected. Their bodies and hearts were healed and they begin to grasp who they were really made to be as Jesus released the Father's Love and spoke identity to them. As Jesus prepared to leave His disciples, He told them He would be praying for them in Heaven and that His Father would send The Comforter to them to intercede for them here on Earth. Jesus equipped the disciples to walk in power and love as they demonstrated Kingdom principles everywhere they went while sharing the Good News that man had been set free from sin and forgiven by our Heavenly Father. Because of Jesus, our struggle is finished - all we need to do is receive the gift of Salvation which Jesus paid for on the Cross and walk in His ways, continuing the work of Our Lord as we release the Kingdom wherever we go.

Jesus is the beginning and the end (Revelation 22:13) – He alone can change hearts, causing us to follow Him and walk in His ways. We should be presenting Him and His hope to those who have not yet received His gift of Love and are still stuck in the world, just trying to make it through another day.

Christ in me – the HOPE of Glory! (Colossians 1:27)

Have you renewed your mind? Have you chosen to be transformed by allowing yourself to believe what Jesus, Father God and the Holy Spirit say about you? Have you been transformed by the washing of the Word? Are you choosing to see yourself as He sees you?

Levels of Foundations

In some instances, those who have just been awakened from their dead life prior to knowing the Lord are still so dry that they can get almost buried by the salt of life which they now encounter. When they try to build a new life in the Lord, they can still be tied to their past and the reliving of it can keep them dry as they try to build a new foundation in the Lord. As a result, they can end up with a foundation built from the ground up which creates prickly areas that are extremely dry and susceptible to collapse. We need to be Spirit-filled so that our salt can be vital, bringing life to others. We need to build a solid foundation, allowing the very breath of God to shape us and bring us more and more alive daily! We also need to immerse ourselves in the Spirit to be Spirit-led and full of life!

Once we have died to self, we can begin to build our foundation on who we are in Christ. We can begin to be the salt of the earth, bringing a refreshing flavor and enhanced vitality to every one we meet. We can bring our light to dark situations as we encourage those who have begun to be overwhelmed by their circumstances. We can be confident that even though we ourselves go through different seasons, the wind and rain and rushing waters of various storms will be used by the Lord to shape us. The rock within each of us is formed in different ways, bringing a unique beauty to each of us, and it continues to develop and change over time. Along the way, we will find safe pastures and oases where we can briefly pause and be refreshed as we adjust to our new growth in the Lord and our overall way of looking upon others will start to reflect His heart of eternal compassion and powerful, everlasting love!

We have all sorts of different geological formations all across this nation which reflect the different ways God has shaped the land over time. Seeing this as we travelled the country caused us to consider the question of what does our spiritual foundation look like? How well established is our foundation? Is it built on something that might slip, like the salt beds in Moab Utah that slipped and liquefied and shifted and caused all sorts of interesting things to happen, or is it a solid foundation? One of the thoughts which occurred was that in Death Valley which is at the lowest point within the United States, there was a lack of water and intense heat, giving really exaggerated conditions. This coupled with the name Death Valley made us think that when a Christian finally comes alive in Christ and comes out of that lifestyle which was leading them towards death as they lived a life of sin, there could initially be such a change in their life that they might realize that their foundation did not have

119

any Spirit to it. Their foundation did not have any water present and the salt which God made them with was no longer any good; it came up and out, raising up a prickly and dry foundation which was tough to walk upon. What we really need at that point as newborn Christians is to actually cultivate our ability to hear the Spirit and to let God breathe on us in order to fully come alive and become Spirit led Christians who are directly impacted by the very breath of God.

As we walk our way out of that valley of death, we can know that God is always with us. As we build the foundation in our new Christian life, we can know He is with us. Psalm 23 assures us of this and it is an incredible promise, even to many people who have not yet been Reborn. It also points to Jesus as our shepherd and it tells us that "you made me to rest" which reminds us of the importance of us resting in the Lord and resting on His promises, trusting that He does have our best interest at heart.

As we begin to come to know the Lord, we have different states of mind, and as we learn how to actually allow ourselves to be transformed by the renewing of our minds, we are easily impressionable. The best thing we can do is to actually stand firm on the fact that even though we may be new Christians, we do hear from God. There is no miniature or baby Holy Spirit. We need to listen to what He says and be obedient. It is good to check our interpretation of what we think He is saying with someone else whom we know is walking with the Lord, but in reality, the final authority for us is God. This can cause us to be uncomfortable at times since God always brings increase and expansion. It can also cause some other believers to question what we are doing, but the most important thing for us is that when Jesus was up on the Mount of Transfiguration, Father God opened the heavens and spoke, saying: "This is my beloved son in whom I am well pleased. Hear Him." We need to focus on hearing the Lord, not man. We need to look to Jesus to see what The Father would have us do in each moment of our new lives as Christians.

The Bible tells us that we behold Him as in a mirror and our ability to see Him (and ourselves) is still distorted by the darkness of this world. Let His light shine in on your heart, penetrating it until it swells full to overflow with His powerful, all encompassing Love which then bursts forth as a mighty rushing river of His Living Water. Allow His Word to transform you – stand upon His promises and His Word…He is not a man that He could or would lie (Numbers 23:19). He loves each and every one with a perfect and everlasting Love. Invite Him in to your heart and make Him Lord of your life and let LOVE become your Master!

Choose to Trust in Jesus

I rest wrapped in your peace, confident that your Son paid the price for everything in my life and confident that you have an incredible plan for my life. A purpose for which you knit me together perfectly as I am. I trust you. I have faith that that what you started you will complete. I trust that I hear your voice, that I hear your heart, that I am following you as you lead me beside still waters. So I rest in you, knowing you are good and knowing that I surely do not yet see everything that is coming forth, however I trust in you. If you, God, be for me what can stand against me? I embrace your grace and actively choose to release grace to others as I step into the purpose for which you called me forth for such a time as this. I incorporate all the lessons of the sadness of my past into how I choose to honor others, preferring them before myself as I equip and build them up in your kingdom.

Love is willing to go
To extravagant lengths
To clean us up,
To polish off the tough
Exterior
In order that
His light
May shine through us
Out into the darkness.

The Lord wants to redeem each and every moment of our past lives within the world to build His kingdom upon The Rock, His Son, Jesus Christ of Nazareth. We all learned how we did not like being treated- being lied to, taken advantage of, not being honored, not being believed, etc. Father God Is gracing us with His grace, mercy, and compassion to equip us to change our own way of embracing others, that we would always receive others with honor as His Sons and Daughters. He is training us to look for Him in each and everyone and to encourage the gifts within others to come forth that we would learn how to walk forward in Unity: one Body led by Jesus who is our head. We follow Him. He is redeeming the stains the world tried to leave on us and giving us His Wedding clothes that we may boldly enter in to His throne of grace, knowing we are His!

Love always welcomes us home,
Wrapping us in His love,
Securing us in His safety
As He prepares
To launch us to foreign shores
Bringing hope to one and all.

The truth is that daily life in the world goes on even as I walk out my Spiritual Destiny with you Lord. I choose to:

Focus on you in all situations.
Believe that you are you and greater is He who is in me than he who is in the world.

Place my faith in you and what you are doing.

Look to you first to see what you want to bring forth and release into each situation.

Advance your kingdom always.

Change the spiritual atmosphere.

Rest in you- for you said "it is finished"!

Believe that you meant it when you said "It is good"!

Release Mercy.

Encounter others with grace for where they are at in their Spiritual Development.

Honor others.

Be a peacemaker.

Worship you with Joy in my heart in ALL things!

Be on fire for you!

Destroy doubt and compromise whenever I encounter them.

Actively pursue and step into the fullness of Jesus Christ of Nazareth.

Celebrate You by sharing the Testimony of Jesus whenever I can!

Love loves us!No exceptions!
Filling us full of His promises
As we come alive,
Stepping into the embrace of a lifetime
Knowing that
Because of Him
We are never alone!

He is Faithful!

The point that I'd really like to make through all of this is concerning God's faithfulness. Even though after giving my heart to Jesus when I was 11, I did not pursue walking with Him, Jesus never left me. He never abandoned me. He never gave up on me. As I look back over my life, I can see how He was always faithful, and He was always true to His promise to "never leave me or forsake me". He was always there when I needed Him even though I was sadly unaware of His presence for a lot of years. In some instances, it almost seemed as if God was gently hedging me in, as if He was actually even protecting me from some of my bad tendencies. Just as He promises, His grace is sufficient! The sooner we learn to actually give control of our lives to Him, the better off we will be. It makes me so sad when I think about what a huge lie satan has perpetrated on people - convincing us that by becoming a Christian we lose something! The only thing we lose out on is Death! Jesus came so that we would have life and life more abundant! There is no loss when we give our lives to Jesus. In fact, what we gain is unfathomable. It is so vast that I don't really believe that our human minds can embrace it.

Keep in mind that I had invited Jesus into my heart when I was 11 and it was 30 some years later when I was talking to my Mom about the Lord. I had always called on the Lord in all of my prayers and never differentiated between any of the aspects of the Trinity. So when I was talking to my Mom, the main point I was trying to make with her was that **God does exist**. God is alive and He loves you. Since it had been so long ago when I had invited Jesus into my heart, I didn't remember whatever it was that I was told at that moment, so I was not in a position to share that with her. Believe me, the enemy has tried to beat me up about that since then, but I believe that God knew my heart and that I did the best that I could with what I had at the time. I also know that God has far more Grace then we could even imagine and definitely more Grace than we have for others. So I believe that my Mom is with God and that she is no longer being tormented by the enemy whatsoever. Hallelujah!

Parkinson's was an extremely difficult thing to watch my Mom experience, as well as to experience myself. When we think of Parkinson's, the most noticeable thing is the symptoms of Parkinson's which include tremors and shaking and the inability to control one's muscular movements. The problem is, Parkinson's encompasses a whole lot more than that. It's what they call a brain disease. When you take somebody who has been completely independent and running their own show for 40 years and you suddenly tell them that they are no longer going to be able to do that, it's difficult to say the least. My mom tended to try to over control the things that were left within her ability to control and so it was a very challenging scenario all around.

I hope when I see Mom again, I can tell her once again how much I love her and ask her forgiveness for not having enough patience with her at times. One of my other major regrets in how I handled the situation with my mother is that after she first agreed to me coming up to be here for her, she then tried to back out of it because I think she realized she didn't want anyone to see her heading downhill. So in order to demonstrate to her that it was important for me to be there, I was always trying to make sure that she saw how busy I was. In retrospect, I wish I had just taken more time to simply sit with her, keeping her company. I can say that there were several occasions when I was able, just by being the giant goofball that I am, to get her to laugh deep, deep, deep healing belly laughter. One such occasion was when she became very concerned because she was having hallucinations. I was trying to reassure her and I told her that I was pretty certain it was just the different medications that she had been prescribed. I offered to go into her medicine cabinet and take one of each pill there and then we would "sit down and compare notes." She thought that was hilarious... I was actually serious, because at that point I was thinking that that would be a good break from the daily grind.

As I said, fortunately I heard God saying: "You need to stick with it - you need to go and be there for her." And so I held firm on my decision to go. Well, Thank You, Lord, because about three weeks after I got there, she actually lost her balance while we were walking in the yard, and sat down abruptly on the grass and in doing so, shattered her lower-most vertebrae. The Doctor said it would take 6 weeks in bed and then she would be better. I found that really difficult to believe, but it turned out they were right! Turned out also that I am not a nurse!! So Mom ended up having to hire a nurse to be with her and take care of her because my bedside manner is just straight-up lacking. We joked about how I went to the "Attila the Hun School of Nursing". How good of God though, to make sure that I was up there and in a position to help her until we got her the professional help she needed! Yet another example of how God was watching out over my life all along, no matter how closely I was or was not walking with Him. His Grace truly is Magnificent!

You Are Never Alone!

Just know that you're never alone.

Never.

I believe each one of us goes through our own season of learning that the church and man can only offer us a minimal semblance of what it is that we need from God. In reality, He really is the only one who Loves us the way He Loves us and He's the only one who could ever Love us in the way that we need to be loved and that's because He knows us through and through and He knows just what we need. May He meet you right in the middle of your moment! May you look up and turn and see Him standing there with His arms wide open, waiting, just waiting for you to notice Him. May you wrap yourself in Him and never be the same again, in Jesus' Name I pray! Amen.

Coming Back to Jesus - 2005

When I met the man who became my husband, he was always talking about Jesus. I give him full credit for my coming back into alignment with Father God's Plan for me to have a relationship with Him through the gift of His Son, Jesus Christ of Nazareth. Way back when I was 11, I had asked Jesus into my heart, but I had no idea of what to do after that in order to actively be a Christian. Back in those days, the phrase that I kept hearing was "Born Again Christian", but nobody said anything more than that. There was no explanation for what that meant. If you were a Christian, you were a Born Again Christian. At least that was my understanding of it.

When I met the man who became my husband, he was emphatic about the importance of Jesus. "Jesus is the only way to enter into a relationship with the Father - there is no other way." Hearing him constantly talk about Jesus and the importance of what Jesus accomplished for us on the Cross, caused me to more fully embrace having Jesus in my life. Over time, I grew more and more passionate about Jesus, Father God and the Holy Spirit. I kept hoping that my husband would join me in my passionate pursuit of Jesus, however for whatever reason, he seemed stuck where he was. I did a lot of praying concerning the subject and the best lesson that I can share with anyone is that the position of our own Heart is of the utmost importance to God; He is concerned with **our** heart not with our opinion concerning someone else's heart. It's possible that when I was praying for my husband, my prayers might have been considered controlling or manipulative because when I'm honest, I must admit that I hoped for a certain outcome from my prayers. In reality, the most valuable prayer is the prayer we pray for someone else's breakthrough simply so that they can enter into their own unique relationship with Jesus and Jesus himself might receive the reward for His suffering. I cannot tell you how many times I have heard Heaven reply "I understand that you feel that's an issue, however, I want to know what you are doing about you and your own breakthrough?"

There will come a day when Father God will ask us what we did with the talents that He gave us, and we will be accountable. He will not ask us "how many people did you pray for who then had breakthrough?" I'm pretty certain He already knows the answer to that question. Along those same lines of discussion, why is it that we sometimes feel it's necessary to let somebody else know that we've been praying for them when they never even asked us to pray? It seems to me that when we do this, we are actually, in an underhanded way, turning the emphasis to what we did for them, instead of trying to build them up, train them, or equip them within their own walk. Anytime that Father God puts it on our heart to pray for someone, He's not doing it so that we can get credit. He's doing it so that we will partner with Him and His plan will come forth and I'm pretty certain that His plan has no big accolade in it for us. His plan is about them and their breakthrough. We just get the opportunity to receive a bonus through partnering with Father God, because no matter what the outcome, we are always improved when we partner with Father God!

The problem with any of our behavior that is controlling or manipulative is that we are once again opening an avenue of attack by satan within our own lives. When we choose to control and manipulate people or events, we are in a sense declaring that our way of doing things is for the best, and that quite clearly is PRIDE. Father God does not like people who are controlling and manipulative. Father God likes people who are obedient and are willing to simply do as He asks without the need for recognition or fanfare. It's time for us to set aside our self-absorption with recognition and simply cherish the opportunity to actually partner with the one true living God who spoke the Universe into existence and lovingly scooped us out of the dirt and then blew His Divine breath into us, giving us life!

Salvation vs Discipling

The Church has gotten off track in our pursuit of expanding the Kingdom. For some reason, we began to believe that the goal was Salvation: getting others "saved". However, Salvation can never really be a goal when it is only by the Grace of God that anyone can receive Salvation (Ephesians 2:9). By definition, a goal is something that you work your way towards. There's nothing that man could ever do to work his way back into right relationship with Father God once man doubted the goodness of God and fell to the temptation of sin the Garden (Genesis 2:16-17).

n reality, what Jesus calls us to is discipling others (Matthew 28:19-20). Salvation is meant to be a vehicle which allows the Christian Believer to become who it is they always wanted to be, but had no ability on their own to become. Jesus leads us through how to overcome sin in order to be transformed. Salvation allows us to learn how it is that God sees us as we read His Holy Bible and then apply His truth to our minds so that we can be transformed (Romans 12:2) as we learn to think in a way that is closer to the way that Father God thinks. The sooner it is that we learn how God sees us, and the possibilities which are available to us through the gift of Jesus, the sooner we are able to begin to become who it is that Father God always intended for us to be.

Light Provokes Darkness

Have you ever met somebody and taken an immediate dislike to them? Only to discover later on that one of the reasons why you didn't like them was that they are so much like you? I believe that the Lord was on to something when He admonished us to address the plank in our own eye before we go after the speck in someone else's (Matthew 7:5). There is a lot of Truth to the idea

hat light provokes darkness - what I mean by this is that
the light could actually be provoking the darkness that is
still hidden in our hearts. Interesting concept. What if
when we encounter someone else who has that same
issue or Familiar Spirit, it actually provokes the still
remnant sliver of darkness which might remain within us
as we are being set free more and more. Since we realize
that we are always in a Realm of Spiritual Warfare, that
Spirit that resides in them is what provokes us, causing us
to react. It's imperative that we pursue our own heart
wholeness and healing, and the only way to do that is by
applying Scripture to our Spiritual malady. Scripture is the
way that Jesus showed us to defeat satan when He was
in the wilderness being tempted and provoked (Matthew
4:1-11). If Jesus relied on scriptural Truth to defeat satan,
why would we be any different? There's such incredible
wisdom in the Scriptures. They shall know the truth and
the truth shall set them free (John 8:32). Even satan, our
outright enemy, knows scripture and that is the only thing
that will free us from him! The Bible tells us to submit
ourselves to the Lord, resist the enemy, and satan shall
flee (James 4:7). It sends him packing!

The idea is to get so much of Jesus into us that when the
world squeezes us, Jesus comes out. We don't want to
continue to fall back into our old default patterns of
behavior because, quite basically they just didn't work.
Instead, we want to reflect Jesus when the world
squeezes us. We want the world to see the testimony of
what Jesus has accomplished in our lives. We want them
to have a chance to experience Jesus through our actions

133

and the way in which we choose to interact with them. The Bible tells us that out of the abundance of the heart, the mouth speaks (Matthew 12:34, Luke 6:45). The key is for us to get so much of Jesus in us that He's what comes out when we're put into stressful situations and the world will then notice the difference in us. When they see the difference in us and they see that we are always trying to interact with others in a loving way, they will know that we are His by the way we love (John 13:35). Eventually they will realize that is what they want in their own lives because Jesus is "the desire of Nations" (Haggai 2:7).

Once we become transformed by washing our minds with the word of God (Ephesians 5:26), we are then able to begin to focus on helping other people to learn who it is that He says they are so that they too may start to live life more abundant in Jesus (John 10:10). One of the greatest things that the Body of Christ could begin to do effectively today is to choose to disciple others. We need to train and equip others so that they can overcome the obstacles in their lives and become who Father God made them to be so that they can step into their proper positions within the Body of Christ and the Body of Christ can then move forward together in unity, following Jesus Christ who is the head (Colossians 1:18)!

Millstone vs Milestone

In the Bible we are instructed that it would be far better for us to *"tie a millstone around our neck"* and throw ourselves into the deep end of the ocean than to risk adversely impacting a small child (Luke 17:2 and Matthew 18:6). We are also warned that teachers are held to a far higher standard than others (James3:1) because of what teachers have been entrusted with. It was very clear that Jesus had no fondness for the way the Pharisees had taken advantage of the people they were supposed to be helping to train up and enlighten and lead (Matthew 23). The Bible also promises us that if we train up children in the way in which they should go, they will not depart from it later on (Proverbs 22:6). It is clear that teaching others concerning spiritual realities and truths is very serious business within the Kingdom of God.

Our biggest challenge may be developing a way to remove ourselves from the influences of the culture within which we are living in order to train and teach people in a Biblical fashion. We need to seek God's heart on strategic teaching within the Kingdom and then implement that as we disciple others. Jesus showed an incredibly courageous model when He was teaching the disciples. In a revolutionary approach, Jesus simply told the disciples that they had been given all they needed to cast out demons and heal the sick - He told them to go and do it! Don't even take a change of clothes! Just go and do it and if you're not welcome somewhere, don't get offended, just take your peace with you and knock the dust off your feet (Matthew 10:14) and know that it's going to be okay. That's not exactly what He said, however, I believe that was the spirit in which He said it. So the disciples headed out, two by two, and they did exactly what Jesus told them they could do! As they were returning to Jesus, they were sharing stories with each other in a bragging manner, trying to decide who had done the greatest miracles. They even discussed one town that had not received Jesus and they asked Jesus whether or not they should call down fire upon that town in order to just remove it from the map (Luke 9). Jesus, at this point, told them *"you're not of the right spirit."* That was it! He did not put them into it a forced timeout. He did not take away their Title of "Disciple". He did not shun them, and most of all, He didn't sever ties with them or denounce them claiming that they were no longer a friend. Instead, Jesus gently put them back on the right track again. No big fanfare. He just set them straight.

Within today's Church, we seem to struggle with this. We've developed all these huge lists of requirements that people have to meet before they're even allowed to participate and work within their giftings. We also have huge, huge requirements for people who have backslidden, in order to make sure that they are properly reintroduced to Christianity. And we have all these manmade requirements which, quite frankly,I don't see within the Bible. I definitely don't see them reflected when I look to Jesus as my example of how to be a "Leader" within the Kingdom. So the question is: are we creating

Milestones that people need to actually accomplish within their Christian walk in order to be recognized in certain positions? Or are we actually creating Millstones for ourselves?

All of these requirements and positions seem to be man-made to me. I am not convinced that they will stand the test of time and endure the fire of God on that day when He burns up all the stubble (1 Corinthians 3:13). I believe that as the Church, and as representatives of the Kingdom of God, we can do better. I believe that there's a way to train people and equip them and teach them in a loving manner that honors who it is that God has made them to be right from day one. I believe that when somebody is baptized with the Holy Spirit, they have the full Holy Spirit - there is no Junior Holy Spirit. I believe that what Jesus accomplished on the Cross most assuredly is good enough for each and every one of us to enter in to our relationship with Him. I believe that those relationships are all unique and that I may not understand someone else's relationship with Him but that's my challenge, not something that they need to correct.

Jesus, The Firstfruits of Many

When we choose to invite Jesus in to our hearts to be our Lord and Savior, ALL of Heaven celebrates (Luke 15:7)!!! Heaven celebrates the unfolding of Father God's Plan - The Plan He birthed before the foundation of the world (Ephesians 1:4)! He is the beginning and the end

(Revelation 22:13) of His Plan! From the very beginning it was about choice - do you choose life through obedience or do you choose to pursue personal knowledge by entering into Rebellion?

We were in Him before He spoke the Universe into existence (Ephesians 1:4) and lovingly made Adam and Eve. He knows everything and He has had a glorious Plan all along! For He is the author and finisher of our faith (Hebrews 12:2) and when we choose to place our trust in Him through faith, we have chosen to become a part of His Plan. When we choose to follow Jesus and allow ourselves to be transformed by the renewing of our minds (Romans 12:2), we have chosen to become partners with Heaven, allowing His Plan to unfold within our lives.

Jesus is and was the first fruits of many (1 Corinthians 15:23) and it is only because He laid His life down that we too can overcome this fallen world. Follow Jesus; follow His example for how to resist the enemy while sharing the Word of your testimony and because of the Power of the Blood of Jesus, you too shall overcome the constraints of your old life, that life that was still ensnared in the grips of the world.

Father God takes great delight in looking upon us as we are transformed more and more into the fullness of Christ. Once we choose to follow Jesus, we are *"hidden in Christ"* (Colossians 3:3). We are also seated with Christ in the Heavenlies (Ephesians 2:6) and have access to the very mind of Christ which equips us to overcome the world while also becoming the world's solution to all sorts of challenges which used to perplex us and eventually defeat us. Because of Christ, we walk in victory - no longer merely being victims of the "storms" of the world. As we access the mind of Christ, renewing our minds, we cannot help being transformed! The Holy Spirit guides us in all truth (John 16:13) and convicts us (John 16:8) of areas where we need to receive and apply the Truth of the Word in our lives. For we shall *"know the truth and the truth shall set us free"* (John 8:32). As we grow in truth, we bear greater and greater testimony to the transformative power of Christ in our lives.

When the Father looks upon us, He sees the effect that His Son, Jesus, our Lord and Savior, has had upon us and this surrender of our lives brings Glory to Jesus. Only Jesus could transform us so gloriously! His Love never fails (Psalm 136)! Truly, the Glory of the Lord is upon us and we shall do even greater things (John 14:12-14) when Jesus Himself is our starting place! As we grow in Christ, His Glory becomes ever more evident within our lives and eventually the entire earth will be covered with the Glory of the Lord (Habakkuk 2:14) as more and more brothers and sisters rise up and let their lights shine (Matthew 5:16). We were made to reflect Christ, the Light of the World (John 8:12), who came to shatter the darkness while undoing the works of evil as we walk in the authority Jesus alone gives us. It is time for us to rise and shine that the whole world will know that the Father so loved that He sent His only begotten Son (John 3:16) to be the first fruits of many (1 Corinthians 15:23).

Jesus Still Heals

Shortly after I returned to Florida in October of 2005, it became clear that I was going to need to have something done about my shoulder. My arm basically just hurt to be a part of my body. The way I would try to describe it to other people was by saying: "it feels like I imagine it might feel if I had been shot." I was able to get an MRI done and I started the process of getting back into the Veterans Administration system in hopes that it might be covered since I remembered injuring it way back when I was in the Military. Unfortunately, since there was no documentation in my record about a shoulder injury, it did not pan out the way I had hoped. However, by going into the VA, I ended up learning about a really good surgeon in the area who sounded like just the person I needed to talk to. I was able to arrange to have the surgery done at an outpatient clinic and since I was self-pay, I was relieved to learn that I had enough money to cover the cost of it. All in all, it cost me $3,000 and A World of Pain! I remember coming to after the surgery, feeling like an animal that had been hit by the side of the road - I actually woke myself up by my screams. My husband took one look at me and turned and said to the Doctors "whatever you gave her before the operation, you need to give her two of them right now and I'm going to go and get her pain medication and then

I'll come back for her." It was not pretty. That first night, the only place I was able to sleep was while trying to go to the bathroom and it seemed like I was up every hour on the hour trying to take more pain medication to stay ahead of the pain because I remembered how bad it it been when I woke up after the surgery. The next day I was counting the pain medication pills to try to figure out how many I had taken and my husband walked in and I think he thought that I liked the pain pills so much that I was trying to see how many I had left. Not the case whatsoever! Those pills hardly even touched my pain. In fact I was so disappointed in their effectiveness that I actually flushed the rest of them the next day. The only thing that medication did was make me feel pathetic. In fact, it made me feel so pathetic that I decided to tell the people at the VA that I was allergic to it so that I would never, ever be prescribed that medicine again!

My shoulder had to be immobilized for an entire month because they had cut a hooked part off the bone and had put in nine permanent stitches because they said that when they went in there, there was a hole the size of the tip of my thumb through the Muscle Band. So I guess my explanation of how it felt was actually pretty right on. To make a long story short, I was up in the middle of the night for quite a few nights, talking to the Lord and thanking him for healing me ahead of time. At one point I ran into the lady who lived across the street from me who was a dedicated Christian. She asked what had happened and I told her the story and she said she would pray that I would be healed quickly. The only strategy I

141

knew was what I had seen on Christian television, so I continued to thank God ahead of time before seeing the healing in its fullness. I didn't have the money to get physical therapy so I was gingerly trying to increase my range of motion once the doctor said that I could start moving my shoulder. Did I mention that my shoulder had been so successfully immobilized by me that I actually started to get frozen shoulder which is a whole other realm of discomfort? In any event, I finally got to where I could raise my hand halfway. After that I just seemed to be kind of stuck at that level of healing. So I continued thanking God ahead of time for the healing.

Suddenly, one day my arm shot straight up and it was completely healed! I thought: "God is so good!" As I was walking around my neighborhood, I ran into the lady from across the street and she asked how I was doing and I told her the testimony of how good God was and she replied "yes, I bet that happened about 2 weeks ago." That caught me off guard because that's exactly when it happened. She then told me that she had been watching the 700 Club and they had called out a healing for someone with excruciating pain in their right shoulder and even though it was the middle of the night and everyone else was asleep, she jumped up and yelled out at the top of her lungs "I claim that healing for Ede, in the Name of Jesus!" That was the day that my arm was completely healed! God is so good!

When I went to see my Doctor next for an updated check on my shoulder, I wanted to share the testimony with him.

I told him: "you probably should have a seat because you're not even going to begin to believe what God did for me." I then showed him that my arm went straight up over my head and that I had full range of motion and he was amazed! I concluded the testimony by telling him how good God was and he said: "you don't even know how good God is." I asked him what he meant. He replied: "I told you before that yours was one of the worst three that I had seen in all my years of doing surgery. What I did not tell you was that yours actually was the very worst. I did not tell you at that time that if you did not have your shoulder done when you did, within a month you would have lost the ability to ever use your arm again and no surgeon could have fixed it!" I said "Wow! God is so good!"

I decided that I should go and share the testimony with the ladies at the front desk so that the people in the waiting room could hear just how good God is. When I was done sharing with the ladies, they said: "You don't even know how good God is because they sold the facility where you had the surgery done and if you had to do it now today, it would cost you three times what it cost you!" To which I replied: "Wow, God is so good!"

I want to encourage you today and let you know that no matter what you're facing, God has you covered. He knew this day was coming from a long, long time ago and He has been preparing your solution. All you need to do is press into Him and ask Him to show you what it is that

you need to do and then just pursue it in Jesus' Name.
Amen

By mid-February 2008, the constant stress within my
marriage had taken an incredible toll on me and my
persistent, chronic cough had developed into full-blown
pneumonia. I tried to get out of having to go to the
Hospital by going to an Urgent Care facility. They did
some testing and gave me an IV and basically told me
that they really recommended that I go to the Hospital. I
did not have medical insurance and did not know how I
would be able to pay for that so I promised them that I
would come back the very next day, whenever they told
me to, for them to check and see how I was doing. When
I went back the next day, they refused to treat me
because the tests showed I was getting worse and worse,
even though they had given me a complete IV the day
before. They insisted that I go to the Hospital and were
planning to call an ambulance for me, however my only
medical coverage was going to be through the Veterans
Administration and ambulances won't take you to the VA.
So I told them I would go home to get my stuff and then I
would go and check myself into the VA.

I went back to my house and I very distinctly remember
looking out over the beautiful woods. I was filled with
peace, but at the same time quietly in my heart saying a
potential goodbye. Deep within, I had an idea of just how
sick I was. My husband drove me to the VA Hospital and I
filled out the paperwork to be admitted to the Emergency

Room along with the paperwork to get back into the VA system. For years I had known that I had the VA as an available resource in my life, having been in the Military, however I truly felt that there were a lot of people who were far, far worse off than I was and I believed it they should have the resources of the VA, not me. In other words, I didn't want to take the medical care that someone who was sicker than I needed. In any event, at this point in my life I needed help and I needed it now!

When they finally admitted me to the ER, I was put in a curtained off section and was waiting to actually see a Doctor when I had a bit of an epiphany. I realize that for every person like me who was finally about to get the medical help that they so urgently needed, there were probably at least a thousand other people on the face of the planet who were not going to get that help, and quite frankly, they were going to die. That was a sobering thought!

So as I talked to the Lord, I told Him that I had had a really good life and that I felt that I had done most of the things that I had wanted to and had been given a lot of opportunities that a lot of other people never have. I continued on to tell the Lord that if it was my time to die, I was okay with it, however, I hoped that He would allow me to look upon His big toe before sending me where I knew I deserved to go. I was keenly aware of the fact that I had not been living as a completely dedicated Christian despite the fact that I had come back to walking with the Lord in a much more active way. I was also keenly aware that I just did not have the strength within me to survive a full encounter with the Lord which is why I asked to simply see His big toe; I felt that was really all that I could handle at the time. I then proceeded to tell the Lord that if it was not my time to die, I believed that if He could just find me a cave for about a week, I thought I could make it. To make a long story short, the Holy Spirit prompted me to casually mention that I may possibly have been exposed to tuberculosis back when I was in the Military and, Voila... I was giving my very own room. My room was actually kind of an isolation chamber where people had to pass through an airlock door to get to me so I had my cave per my request. God is good!

When I was in the VA Hospital, I was once again trying to use the strategy that I had heard about on many of the Christian TV shows I had watched. I simply lay there, resting, thanking God by saying: "Thank you Jesus for healing me. It is by your stripes that I am healed." For the first two days I pretty much satisfied myself by saying that non-stop while resting. Nurses would come in periodically and take my vitals and when I would ask, they would give me five sets of pajamas because each night I was sweating through 5 complete sets of pajamas and that saved them from having to come in and out all the time.

The really wonderful thing was my Nurses names were Hope, Faith, and Mercy! So whenever these ladies came in, I would talk with them about the Lord and about how I had faith in Him and how much I loved Him and all of the new things that I was learning as a growing Christian and it was quite enjoyable, as far as being in the Hospital goes. At this particular point in time, the inner lobby of the VA was undergoing a large renovation process and I believe they were actually even giving the front of the building a "facelift" as well. They would do a lot of the work during the nights, and there were all sorts of hammerings and loud noises and oddly enough, these noises were very similar to what I heard non-stop for 6 months when I was on the ships that I had served on. A lot of hollow, metallic echoing noises. Well on the second night, I guess I finally fell asleep, and I had this really radical dream. In my dream, I found myself dressed in khaki standing on the Bridge of a ship. I was looking out the front of the ship, over the sea, and the Skipper of the ship was at the announcement panel and had just pulled the Abandon Ship Alarm. Next thing I knew, I was out of my body and I was about 50 feet away from the ship, looking at the ship and it was at that "Titanic Moment" where the bow was underwater and the stern was up above the water and you could see the propeller of the ship exposed. The ship was definitely going to go down! Next thing I knew, I was back on the Bridge and the water was up to my ankles and everybody was running like mad, away from the Bridge of the ship, even the Commanding Officer, as the Abandon Ship Alarm was sounding loudly. I then heard the audible voice of God, asking me: "Are you going to go down with the ship or are you going to walk on water?" I immediately took a huge, exaggerated step forward, indicating that I was going to walk on water! The dream ended and I woke up thinking well that was really a crazy dream! In one sense, I put the dream off to the sounds that I was hearing in the night as they were working on the inner Lobby and the front of the VA building. But I think deeper down in my Spirit, I knew there was a far greater significance to the dream.

The next day as I lay in my bed still just resting, I felt God touch the center of each of my hands with His bright, white, light of Love - that same Love that I had been filled with many years earlier - and it almost felt as if there was a bumblebee inside my two hands that were together as if I were praying. It felt like the Bumblebee started going in circles, getting bigger and bigger and bigger, and quite frankly, I actually felt my body come back to life! You see when I went in to the hospital my entire right lung was full of fluid and 2/3 of my left lung was full of fluid and the Doctors could hardly believe that I had actually walked in to the Emergency Room. So as my body came back to life, I realized just how close I had come to dying.

After eight full days in the hospital, I was released, however they did make me take a small oxygen tank with me because my oxygen saturation level was about 89% which is pretty low and so they wanted to make sure that I was able to get enough oxygen. It actually took a while for them to process me to go home because they could not figure out how to get the oxygen for me with me paying for it and how to reflect that on the paperwork because the particular category of disability that I come under was a rare category for them to encounter. The wonderful thing is that because of being a disabled veteran and not having employment at the time, all of my medical treatments were given to me free of charge. So my entire Hospital stay was completely free! Go God!

When I went to visit my Doctor for my first follow on visit, I was amazed to learn that her first name was Comfort! She was actually from Africa and was a Resident at the University of Maryland which is where the VA receives their doctors from in Baltimore, Maryland. So that was pretty interesting; my Nurses names were Hope, Faith and Mercy and my Doctor's name was Comfort! God is good! During that follow-on visit with my Doctor, she was looking at my record and became very disturbed because she saw that according to my record, nobody had checked my vital signs for the first whole 24 hours that I was in there. I told her that that wasn't possible because there were three Nurses in there on and off with me. She said "Well, that's weird because nobody wrote anything down about your vitals." I repeated to her that Hope, Faith and Mercy were in the room with me. She told me "I don't really know how well you are recalling things, because we don't have any Nurses by those names that I know of." Well that got my curiosity going! As soon as I was done with my appointment with her, I went upstairs to the floor that I had been on and went to the front desk. I told the woman there that I wanted to thank my Nurses from when I had recently been in the Hospital there and I was hoping to speak with Hope, Faith and Mercy. She looked at me in a confused way and told me that there were no Nurses that she was aware of with those names. I honestly didn't really know what to do with that because I didn't have a grid for understanding that because I had not yet at that point been taught about the Supernatural Nature of Father God, Lord Jesus, and the Holy Spirit. Remember, I was just a beginner at this Christian thing! Eager to learn though!

The Downside to Free Will

God made man and gave him the gift of Free Will. God's plan has always been to confound the wise by using the foolish (1 Corinthians 1:27) - God's plan is that Satan will learn once and for all that man would never choose to worship him if he knew what Satan was really all about. Man was made to worship God and to have a relationship with God and to walk with God. God is the one who gives man his worth as well as his identity. Satan was devastated when he saw the loving way in which man was scooped out of the dirt and had divine breath of God breathed into him in order to bring him alive. Ever since that moment, satan has made it his goal to undermine man's relationship with God. God is all knowing. God knows the beginning from the end (Isaiah 46:10). God knows that man will always choose Him, and because of His knowledge of how He made man to be, as well as His knowledge of the beginning from the end, so to prove it, God chose to give man free will.

The problem, or the downside to free will, is that in order for someone to truly make a choice they should be thoroughly educated. satan knows that anyone who is ruly educated and knows the Truth will be set free from his snare, so he won't risk allowing man to simply make his choice. Rather, satan always tries to undermine the Truth and hedges his bets - he has created counterfeits and deceptions all throughout the ages in order to counteract man's ability to choose correctly. Because of free will, God cannot on His own reveal the Truth to people; He cannot simply raid the enemy camp. He cannot on His own rescue man from satan's snares. Free will mandates that someone must choose to partner with God in order to establish what the Truth is or to teach people and educate people on what the Truth is so that they can make a well-informed choice on their own, of their own free will. This is why intercession is so imperative within our spiritual development. We need to continuously be interceding for those who don't yet know the Lord. We need to ask Jesus to go into the heart of the enemy camp and reveal His heart to people who have been ensnared by satan's shame tactics. We need to ask God to reveal the Truth to people whom satan has appeared to disguised as an angel of light (2 Corinthians 11:14) so that they would know the truth and the truth would set them free (John 8:32). A good example of the importance of this is that my husband believed that he saw Jesus and that Jesus told him he was "a worm". In order to get clarification, I asked him: "do you mean that you were in the presence of Jesus and you felt like you were worm or you became aware of just how lowly you were?" My husband said: "No, I saw Jesus and He told me I was a worm." I replied, "that's not Jesus." However, my husband really and truly believed that he saw Jesus and that Jesus told him he was a worm. Well, if Jesus tells you you're a worm, what kind of an invitation to the Kingdom is that? I know that was a deceptive encounter with satan masquerading as an angel of light. So my fervent prayer is:

Lord, if there's anyone who might go to hell because they felt they were condemned through a false encounter with satan masquerading as an angel of light, Lord Jesus Christ of Nazareth, I'm asking that you would reveal yourself to them right now that they would know that you didn't come to condemn them but you came to set them free. You came to show them love and the possibility of life more abundant and the promise of eternal life with you, Jesus. So in the mighty Name of Jesus I ask that you would reveal Your true heart to them, Lord, that they would know the truth and the truth would set them free in Jesus' Name. I asked that more brothers and sisters would represent you well by becoming true Ministers of Reconciliation and Ambassadors for Heaven so that those people who have been shamed by the Church as well as the Spirit of Religion and those who have been deceived through false encounters with an angel of light would come to know your heart Lord and they would know the truth and the truth would set them free in Jesus' Name I pray, Amen.

As we all know, light shatters darkness. What I think we sometimes don't realize is the level at which light aggravates darkness beforehand. The more I got lit on fire for Jesus by attending all of the Christian Conferences

152

that I went to and doing Street Ministry in the Inner City on a daily basis, the darker my husband got. He actually started accusing me of being involved with another man. He kept asking me: "Who is he?! What's his name?" To which I replied: "His name is Jesus and He says He misses you." Seriously. That went over like a lead balloon. It was the truth though and the truth could have set him free (John 8:32) had he chosen to receive it.

You see sometimes that's the key question, are we actually willing to receive what Jesus has for us and act upon it? Christianity is not something that one can simply talk about. God wants us to experience Him and His great Love for us. He doesn't want us to just talk about how we believe He is. That's why the Bible tells us that *"they overcame by the Blood of the Lamb, the Word of their Testimony, and not loving their (old) lives unto death"* (Revelation 12:11). The key is that we need to be willing to be changed by the Bible. We need to be willing to see what it is that the Holy Spirit is pointing out for us to address within our daily lives so that we can come into alignment with who God made us to be. The only way that we can do this is to actually work towards renewing our minds by reading what God says and refusing to continue to listen to what the world says! That is how we are transformed. But it's something that we need to participate in. No one else can do it for us. There were many times when my husband would say that he wished he had grown up in a Christian family. One time I actually weighed in on that subject and asked him what made him think that if he couldn't grab ahold of it today or

153

understand it today that he would have grabbed it or understood it when he was 12 years old?

In retrospect, I believe what he really meant was that he wished somebody else had disciplined him into developing good Christian habits. But that's not how this program works! That's not how Christianity Works. Christianity is available for each and every person and it probably looks different for each and every person because we are designed to be the Body of Christ all together and each one of us has a completely separate function and role and it is only when we are all in our proper positions that the Body of Christ can walk forward in unity, following the head who is Jesus (Colossians 1:18).

The Rainbow Flag

When I was growing up, I went to the Parochial School that was attached to the Church that was at the bottom of the block that we lived on. When I returned there to help my Mother as she was finishing her life on Earth, I discovered that that particular Church was flying a rainbow flag. I didn't have a huge problem with it at the time because I was not yet a fully Bible-believing Christian at that point and having experienced God's Love, I believed that He Loved all of His children equally. At that point in time, I had mistakenly equated Love with accepting everything that one did. I realized later on that, yes, God does Love all of His children. He Loves us so much that He doesn't want us to stay the same that we were on the very first day that He entered our lives. He Loves us so much that He wants us to take in His Truth every chance we get so that we can be transformed from Glory to Glory. He Loves each and every one of His children, however, there are some things that we do that He is not that keen on.

In any event, whenever I thought about that rainbow flag flying on that Church, I would get irritated by the compromise that I felt it represented. When I would attend the church, which was only once or twice to be honest, the very first announcements that they made were concerning the Gay Men's Choir and it was clear to me that their first priority was homosexuality, not God. So I kept telling my friends that: "one of these days I'm going to climb up, rip that flag down and light it up on those front steps of that Church!" My friends all advised against this course of action. Thank you, Jesus, for true friends and wise counselors.

Anyway, one time when I was driving to the town in which I grew up, in my mind I was having a conversation about how I was going to tear down that flag when much to my amazement I heard the Holy Spirit say "Instead of just flapping your lips about it, why don't you actually do something?" Wow, that was a novel concept. Okay, Holy Spirit, what would you like me to do? "Why don't you go and talk to the man?" Wow, this could be a little bit more than I bargained for, I thought. So when I got to my house, I decided that the very least I should do was go prepared with some Scriptures. So I looked up an Old Testament Scripture and a New Testament Scripture covering what my concerns were. I figured that way I was armed because I could demonstrate that in both Testaments of the Bible, God was not keen on homosexual acts. The Holy Spirit then gave me the strategy of sharing my unique Testimony with the man in order to debunk the possibility of him writing me off as a "Homophobe". The beauty of the Holy Spirit's Plan was this: the background behind my coming into existence was due to my uncle's suicide attempt based upon him trying to come to terms with being homosexual while attending West Point. Talk about a difficult circumstance! When my Natural Mother found out that her brother had tried to commit suicide, she ended up getting more involved with the young man she was traveling with than she might have intended to otherwise and - voila, here I am, an unexpected souvenir from her trip to England during her Junior year of College.

So that Sunday morning, I went down to Church and sure enough the first announcements were about the Men's Choir meeting. After the service was over, I took my shoes off and I walked barefoot around the sanctuary three times, reclaiming it for God and then I did the same around the outside of the building. I really felt that it needed to be reclaimed for the Lord and His purposes. It was His building! After that I went up and spoke with the Secretary and told her that I had a problem and I wanted to speak to the "Father" about it. She went and got him

and he invited me into his office. I told him that before I
got into talking about what my problem was, I wanted to
give him a little bit of my background. I then told him that
the way I came into being was that my Mother was on a
Junior year abroad and got word that her brother had tried
to kill himself because he was struggling as a young man
at West Point coming to terms with his homosexuality. I
told him that my Mother got intimately involved with her
traveling partner and that I was the result of that union. I
then told him that based upon the history of my origin, it
was clear that I could not possibly have anything against
homosexuals because "without you guys I would not be
here." Truly! I then told him that I believed that the Holy
Bible was God's inspired Word and that every word within
the Bible was in there for a reason and that God was the
same today as He always ever was and always ever
would be. I continued on to say that based upon the
Scriptures (Leviticus 18:22 and 1 Corinthians 6:9-10),
when I read them, I was concerned for his Salvation.
He replied, "Well, let me share some of my life with you
so that you can better understand me." He told me that he
had hated himself day in and day out for 40 years and
then suddenly one day he heard God say that it was okay
and that He loved him. The "Father" continued on to ask
me "What if God actually brought you down here so that
you could learn something from me?" rather than the case
of me being there to help him learn something. I replied
that all things are possible, however, I don't think that's
the case. He told me that he would be interested to see
what my actions would be when I left, having not
succeeded in converting him over to seeing things my

way, because the last two ladies who tried to change him had cursed him when it did not work. I told him that they clearly had not been sent by the Lord because I could only see two courses of action upon leaving: one would be to knock the dust off my feet and never return again, and the other would be to pray with him. I told him I was going to choose to pray with him. He received my offer to pray, and I prayed a Blessing over him, thanking God for all the lives that were going to be changed as he shared his testimony of what God was going to do for him and others, in Jesus' Name, Amen. I then left.

As I walked back up the street to my house, I found myself thinking how glad I was that conversation was over. I had gone there prepared with only two Scriptures, trusting that the Holy Spirit would tell me what to say and when to say it. I was amazed at the conversation that I had had with the "Father", because the Holy Spirit had given me all sorts of Scriptures that I did not even know that I knew as we spoke back and forth concerning the subject of homosexuality. I believe that throughout that conversation I demonstrated the love that Jesus asks us to show one another on His behalf. I felt like I had really accomplished something by planting the seeds that were planted and then praying the prayer that the Lord led me to pray, blessing him.

As I walked up the street to my house, I started thinking about how glad I was that that was over so that I could now smoke some pot and feel better, more relaxed. And as I started thinking about that, I very clearly heard the

Holy Spirit say: "Are you kidding me? You just told him to clean out his closet and now you're just going to go on with life as usual? Do you think that God only wants to use you from 9 to 5? How effective of a minister can you be if you're high?" All valid questions.

As I walked up the front steps to the house, I realized that I had smoked the last marijuana that I ever intended to smoke. When I entered the house, I searched it like I'd never searched it before and I took every single thing that I found and flushed it all down the toilet. I then proceeded to read the entire Gospel of John over the next few days and in doing so grabbed ahold of the full nature of our Inheritance in Christ. I was amazed by Jesus's prayer concerning us: that we would be in Him and Him in us as He is in the Father and the Father is in Him. I was amazed that Jesus gave us the Glory that His Father gave Him that we would walk in His ways, giving even more Glory to His Father!

I have to say that my life was profoundly changed from that moment forward and I have never looked back! You see, I know what I have been forgiven of and I know what Jesus experienced on the Cross for me and I know that it is only by the Grace of God that I am alive. Seriously, the odds were against me even being born to begin with. I was born to an unwed Mother back in the early sixties and it definitely would have been far easier for her to just quietly get an abortion then to carry me to term and then go through the heartbreak of giving me up to strangers whom she never met. She even forfeited attending her

Senior year of College to hide in a hot apartment while pregnant with me until it came time for her to travel to another State where she had me. Years later when I was reunited with her, she told me that the only way she got through that was by imagining in her mind that she was giving me back to God because she knew that I was a gift from God right from the very first moment she found out she was pregnant. I believe that her giving me back to God and her fervent prayers on my behalf every day after that are some of the things that kept me from completely derailing my own life as I made some less-than-ideal choices while navigating doing things my way before I came back to Christ.

Learning in Person How Light Provokes Darkness

As I continued to get to know Jesus, I got so lit on fire for Jesus that my husband could only stand to be around me for a couple of weeks at a time and then he would jump in the car and drive up to see his mother for a couple weeks and then he would come back and it was just back and forth like a ping pong ball. Eventually I realized that there was something that was exceedingly unhealthy within our relationship and it didn't seem that it was going to change. It seems to me that the vast majority of his frustration was because my husband felt that he was not "in control" of his own life. So since he seemed to have a big long list of reasons why he could never just take a moment and enjoy life with me, I thought maybe if we just took the whole challenge of our marriage out of the equation for a little while, he could take charge of the other areas of his life and when he felt like he had some semblance of control going on in his own life, we would then readdress the issue.

I have to confess that a lot of my time in those days was spent doing whatever I could to make sure that our marriage didn't end up on his list of problems within his life. In retrospect, I realize that by doing that, by running interference, I actually prevented him from ever having to make a choice to fully invest in our marriage, period, to actually choose our marriage over everything else in his life. That was wrong. And I believe that's one reason why it was so easy for him to just hop in his car and drive off whenever the going got tough in his mind. In any event, as soon as I realized that there was an exceedingly unhealthy dynamic in operation within our marriage, I also realized that I'm not a Co-Dependent and so I talked with him and told him that I thought we needed to separate. In Maryland the paperwork that you file to be legally separated is called filing for "Limited Divorce" and of course when he received those papers, he didn't believe for a second that I didn't intend to fully divorce him after the year of being separated was completed. So he returned the favor and sued me for divorce, that would be "Absolute Divorce", claiming that I was involved in an adulterous relationship.

161

Imagine my horror - first and foremost, as a Christian I was getting a Divorce, and secondarily I was being accused of adultery when in reality the only person I was engaged with and actively involved with was Jesus! It would actually be kind of funny if it wasn't so tragically sad. Imagine how he must have felt if he really believe that... The things that the enemy was telling him must have really hurt a lot.

As I navigated the process of getting divorced while being a Christian, there were plenty of people who wanted to pray for me and the strategy that the Holy Spirit showed me was to simply say to them: "I'm not entirely certain what God is doing in this instance, therefore, if you could please simply pray in tongues for me that would be wonderful!" There are many times when those closest to me would tell me how much they wished they could spare me what I was going through. But in looking back on it, I would not be the woman I am today or have the depth of relationship with Jesus that I have today had I not gone through that long, dark Valley. I don't believe anybody else on the planet could have pushed me as readily into the arms of Jesus!

So, not only did my husband introduce me to the vital importance of Jesus within the Christian walk, he was then pivotal in helping me to develop an extremely deep relationship with Jesus. As crazy as it sounds, I thank God on a daily basis for my husband and I thank God for the Grace and the Mercy that He has for my husband.

One of the important things that the Lord showed me was that given the level of opposition that my husband experienced, he must have an incredible Destiny in the Lord and I know that the Body of Christ cannot move forward together in Unity until everyone is within their proper position. I do not want to be the elder brother who begrudged the prodigal as he returned to the Father's good graces, rather I want to celebrate whatever the position is that my husband has, knowing that he is uniquely qualified to reach people who have had a really tough time in their lives. As I was coming to terms with all of these things, my great friend Lorraine would say that she wished she could spare me what I was going through. I would always reply to her: "Yes, but look at who it is that I am today because of all these things. I would not be the same person without having worked my way through this!" I believe at times, as people, when our friends are going through things we might be tempted to pray a prayer like: "God, rescue them! Take them out of that situation!" when in reality, we should be praying: "Lord, may they get everything that you have for them within that situation and may they get it quickly, in Jesus' Name! Amen."

The best advice I could give anyone when considering marrying someone and spending the rest of their life with them would be to pay particular attention to how the person acts and responds in stressful situations. One of the biggest mistakes I ever made in my life was excusing poor behavior by thinking "well, they were just stressed". No! Stress reveals true character because at that point pretenses can't be maintained. I'm not saying to set out to provoke others, but I am saying pay attention. Stress does reveal true character - it's when people are caught off-balance that they can no longer pretend to be who they think you want to see. The most important thing ever for you to know about someone you are considering spending the rest of your life with is that they have an upstanding and upright, true morally sound character, so keep your eyes open and don't make excuses for their poor behavior.

The Transformation of Saul Into Paul

Until he encountered Jesus on the road to Damascus, Saul thought he was defending his faith by killing Christians. Once Jesus revealed His heart to him, Saul was forever changed. Initially Saul was blinded by the Glory of the Lord, then days later as promised by the Lord, the scales fell off of his eyes and he was a "new man". His name was even changed to Paul and he began to travel from City to City, giving the incredible testimony of his transformation from a misguided murderer of the Brethren into a completely dedicated Apostle, preaching the Gospel everywhere the Holy Spirit led him to go. Paul epitomized the scripture which declares *"If any man be in Christ Jesus, he is a new creation. All things are made new"* (2 Corinthians 5:17).

The vast majority of the New Testament is believed to be the writings of Paul, encouraging and instructing the young Churches that were planted as the Apostles traveled around testifying to the continued works of Christ. Paul declared *"I am convinced nothing can separate us from the love of God in Christ Jesus, neither death nor life, nor angels nor rulers, nor things present nor things to come, nor powers nor height nor depth, nor anything else in all creation"* (Romans 8:38). This is good news indeed! If God can transform a murderer into His number one spokesperson, there is certainly hope for us to be of use, especially since love never fails and Jesus Christ Himself promised He would never leave us nor forsake us!

God Made Us to Walk Upright

Father God made us upright and upstanding, balanced on two feet. He made us with arms to reach out to others with and hands to touch others with as well as give generously with. He gave us eyes to see with so that we can see who He directs us towards as we walk along the path He has for us, reaching all those whom He places in front of us.

He gave us eyes that we may read His Word, The Living Word, that we will be activated by it as we are nourished by the "Bread of Life". Jesus declared *"man does not live by bread alone but by every word from the mouth of the*

165

Father" (Matthew 4:4). We need to ask the Lord to speak to our hearts that our hearts would be His and our eyes would see what He wants us to see and focus upon. When our eyes are closed, we are in darkness so we need to ask the Lord to open our eyes that we might serve others as we allow the light which the Lord has placed within us to shine outward, scattering the darkness.

The Lord gave us ears to hear with so that we may listen to His Word for that is how faith comes (Romans 10:17). The Bible tells us that as His sheep, we know His voice. It is imperative that we take time to listen to what our Lord has to say to us, what He wishes to share with us. Any strong relationship is defined by effective communication skills; this involves speaking as well as actively listening. We need to develop our ability to hear and recognize His voice as we grow as Christians. We also need to learn how to open our hearts and Minds as we learn more and more about our Lord, Jesus Christ, Our Savior, and His thoughts about us as well as His plans for us. Our heavenly Father wants us to walk with Him on a daily basis!

Father God made us with a mouth; He actually breathed life into us through our mouth. We breathe and eat through our mouth - we are nourished through it. We are also able to "nourish" others by speaking and sharing the word of God with them. The power of the spoken word can never be overstated...the entire Universe was spoken into existence by Almighty God, our Heavenly Father, and our Bible says that His word never returns empty without accomplishing that for which it was sent (Isaiah 55:11)!

God designed us to walk, balanced, on two feet, grounded to the Earth with our heart and our head aimed towards heaven. We are *"seated in Heavenly places in Christ Jesus"* (Ephesians 2:6) and have access to the mind of Christ. We are in the world, but are not of this world (John 17:14), because Jesus overcame the world that we might have life more abundant (John 10:10).

Renew Your Mind and Be Transformed

As long as we simply continue on as we always have, just living our lives while minding our own busy-ness, the enemy is still succeeding. Sure, we will eventually go to Heaven some day in the "by and by", but is that really fulfilling God's Plan for us or the Kingdom?

What about being "transformed from Glory to Glory (2 Corinthians 3:18)"? Did you notice that our starting place is GLORY?! God never intended for us to simply survive, one day miraculously actually making it into Heaven. The Kingdom is NOT a physical destination – it is a way of living life, truly entering in to life MORE abundant (John 10:10), TODAY!

What about choosing to be *"transformed by the renewing of your mind"* (Romans 12:2)? Simple, but not always easy, for satan will question our faith every step of the way..." Did He really say that?" Or "Who do you think you are? Don't you remember how you totally blew it back when you...?" Anything negative or about our past is the enemy trying to re-establish prominence in our heads. After all the real battleground is in our thought life, that is why the Bible admonishes us to *"take every thought captive to the obedience of the Lordship of Jesus Christ"* (2 Corinthians 10:5). It is also why the Bible instructs us to put on the helmet of Salvation as we put on our Spiritual Armor each day (Ephesians 6).

Have you been forgiven by what Jesus accomplished and paid for for you on the Cross? Have you forgiven yourself? If the Lord of Glory says: *"Forgive them, they know not what they do"* (Luke 22:34), **receive it**! Seriously, think about it, even Saul of Tarsus was forgiven, and then his name was changed to give him a fresh start!

Don't rent space in your head to the enemy any longer!

Jesus paid dearly for ALL of you – mind, soul, spirit and body! It is time to actually submit to the Lordship of Jesus in our lives. Let Him heal your broken areas – He is the Master Physician (John 5:1-9) and He already knows exactly what each of us needs. He has a Plan and it is a truly a glorious one. Receive it!

If there is a temptation you are experiencing, or an old habit that you have been convicted of by the Holy Spirit, et Jesus lead you to freedom! He says: "Follow me" and He gives great examples of how we can follow Him straight into a new life by overcoming this world. After He was water Baptized and the Holy Spirit landed upon Him, Jesus was led into the wilderness (Matthew 4:1) where He was tempted by satan as He fasted for forty days, growing closer to His Father through prayer, fasting, and worship. After He ended His fast, satan returned to tempt Him again. Jesus overcame the temptation of this world by the Word of God to which even satan had to bend his knee, recognizing the truth (Matthew 4).

The most effective way to defeat the enemy's attempts to derail our Christian walk through temptation is through the Word of God. We can release scripture over our lives, declaring boldly, *"I can do all things through Christ Jesus who strengthens me"* (Philippians 4:13). Or saying: *"Greater is He (Jesus in my heart) who is in me than he who is in the world (satan tempting me)"* (1 John 4:4). For God's Word never goes forth without accomplishing that for which it was intended – it never returns void (Isaiah 55:11 and 46:10 and Proverbs 30:5).

Sharing The Lord with Others

Having been thumped upside the head by many a well-intentioned religious zealot, I knew that I did not want to ever do that to someone else once I became a Born Again Christian. It actually created a dilemma within me because I did not want to deny Jesus, but I also didn't want to ever treat someone the way I had been treated. The problem is that when someone is led by a Religious Spirit, their focus is on sin and the fact that a person is living a completely messed up life. Well, I already knew my life was off track. I certainly didn't need them to point it out to me and to be quite honest, they weren't going to earn any points with me when they did point it out.

Each person has to get to where they want Jesus, not necessarily a place of where they are terrified of impending doom because of their actions. When a person is dangled over the pit of Hell and threatened with eternity there, sure, they recognize that they need Jesus and that they can't get themselves out of that situation on their own. The problem though is that that's not a conversion that takes. It's not a conversion that causes them to experience the goodness of God and it's the goodness of God that leads to repentance (Romans 2:4). It's only when we repent that we truly change the way we look on things and that is what leads to a change in our actions. That is what it takes for someone to truly become a Born Again Christian.

As I wrestled with my dilemma, I heard the Lord say to me: "What is it that you are really concerned about?" My initial answer was: "What will they think of me?" And then the great realization struck: if I was talking to people on the streets of the inner city, the greatest likelihood was that I would never ever see the person again. If I were to see the person again, more than likely it would be in

Heaven and I'm pretty sure then in that case they would be extremely happy to see me again. With that one simple revelation, my dilemma disappeared - kind of like the vapor that our lives on Earth are (James 4:14) ... This is just a short moment in time, not Eternity.

Once I got beyond that challenge, the next crucial step in my evolution as an Evangelist was to come up with a lead-in, or a "tag line" that would buy me enough time to actually hear what it was Heaven wanted me to say to each person I interacted with. You see as I do Street Ministry, I never fully know exactly what it is the Lord wants to bring forth in each encounter with others. In some instances, I will get a Word of Knowledge about a pain that they are suffering from or a Word of Knowledge concerning the way life has treated them, and in other instances the Lord will give me a glimpse as to how He sees them which can then be offered to them as an invitation to Journey with Him as they pursue that potential in their lives. There have even been times when I thought I was going to say one thing as I approached someone, and then much to my amazement, I heard something completely different come out of my mouth. That is when you know it truly is the Holy Spirit!

In any event, the lead-in line that the Lord gave me was something like this: "This may sound strange to you, but as I saw you, I felt like I heard the Lord say..." Or the Lord might cause me to say "Do you by any chance have a pain in your blank? The reason I ask is because the moment I saw you, I experienced pain there and I don't have pain there. So when that happens, I know that the Lord is letting me know that there is someone I'm going to encounter who suffers from that and He wants to heal them so it wouldn't have been right of me to simply walk past you if it was you that had that pain."

There was actually one day when I was walking in my neighborhood in Utah and I had significant pain in one of my feet so I resolved to share that with every single person I saw on my walk. I went up to six different people, even flagged down the Water Bottle Delivery Man - I flagged his truck down because I saw him twice and figured there was a reason for that - yet none of those people had a pain in their foot. In each instance, I explained why I was asking them and then I asked them if I might pray a blessing over them and continued on my way. After about the third or fourth person, I looked up at Heaven and I said: "Lord, I have absolutely no problem if you simply just want to teach people in this neighborhood that you care enough to heal people today. I will still be faithful and give this Word of Knowledge to each person I see." Right as I said that, I saw a red bird flying overhead which filled my heart with happiness because I love Cardinals. So I took that as a "God wink" and continued on my walk. There were still no takers for the pain in the foot, but I was faithful and I shared that God heals today with every single person I ran into. I have to admit that I got some interesting reactions to each short encounter, but I was faithful.

Finally, as I was turning to come home, I saw a little lady in her garage sweeping so I went up to her and - voila - it was her! I asked her if I could pray with her and she said yes and so I did. The Lord healed her hurt foot and I then asked her if I could pray a blessing over her and I did and then we hugged and I left. For me, the most interesting thing about the whole experience was that when I got home I looked up whether or not there are Cardinals in Utah, and basically, they do not naturally occur here. So I knew it was a "God wink". He knows just how to encourage us at every turn!

I really found that the most challenging aspect of doing Street Ministry was accomplished once I got comfortable with a lead-in line for each interaction. For me, simply by stating that "This may sound very strange to you, but..." somehow that did away with any need for me to think about how it might seem strange to them because I'm the one who told them it might seem strange so it didn't come from them, it came from me. Hah! In other words, I no longer had to worry about what they would think because I'm the one who pointed it out to them that it might seem strange so that defeated that particular tool for discouragement commonly used by satan... It rendered him and his teammates completely ineffective!

Partner With The Lord of the Harvest

We are at a critical time in the History of Christianity. We are on the eve of the greatest Harvest ever and we are poised on the very edge of the greatest outpouring of Father God's Spirit! However, before we can successfully bring in the Lord's Harvest, we need laborers (Luke 10:2). We need to partner with the Lord and take those He sends to us "under our wing" to disciple them. We will need trained, healed and equipped laborers to disciple the upcoming Harvest. There will be more than enough work to go around so we needn't worry about losing our "Position" to someone else.

Let's just agree to submit to His Lordship and partner with Him to disciple the Laborers He is bringing into His Kingdom to help us with the Harvest. After all…He is LORD of the Harvest!

Welcoming and Discipling the Harvest

The Lord's Ways are higher than our Ways (Isaiah 55:9). He is doing a new thing! No eye has seen, nor ear heard, nor the heart of man imagined what it is that The Lord is preparing for those that Love Him (1 Corinthians 2:9) He told us to pray for Him to bring the laborers *"for the harvest is ripe but the workers are few."* (Luke 10:2 and Matthew 9:37) He warns us over and over to not judge others for as we *"measure so shall we be measured."*

174

Matthew 7:2) He warns us that we cannot see others as we should because as we go after the speck in someone else's eye we really should look to the plank in our own eye (Matthew 7:5) because it blocks our ability to see others as we should.

He tells us we need to *"grow in grace"* (2 Peter 3:18) for freely we received His grace and we should freely give (Matthew 10:18) it to others. He tells us that only He knows the condition of the heart of another (Romans 2:2). How many people have we hurt by judging them based on their appearance alone? What if we prayed for The Lord of the Harvest to send the workers and He sent them only to have us refuse to receive them because they did not look like we thought they should? What if instead of offering grace and looking for His treasure in their hearts and encouraging them to become who He made them to be, we simply met them with hard-hearted judgment? What have we done with the talents He has given us- Have we invested hope in others, knowing that His grace is sufficient ? If we chose grace, might it just be that He could touch them and work a "miracle" in them just as He did in us?

What if He has been answering our prayer to send the laborers all along but we have missed it because we have been preoccupied with our own thoughts on how the laborers should look and as we judged them and dismissed them as having no value to us as they were, we too may be found to be lacking on judgment day. What have we invested in others?

175

Have we spent our talents on teaching others of His never ending Love? Are we going to act like the elder brother when the prodigal brother comes home (Luke 15:11-32)? He had been with the Father all along yet did not understand the Compassionate Love of the Father. He was not willing to invest his inheritance in celebrating the return of his brother who had slipped away. What if it is only someone who has been judged and found wanting by man yet knows they are completely loved by the Father that is able to minister to the people The Lord is drawing into His heart at this time? We need to ask The Lord to search our hearts for any tares that have grown amongst the seeds He planted in our hearts. (Matthew Chapter 13)

We thought we came first in His affection, however He tells us that *"the first shall come last and the last shall come first"* (Matthew 20:16). What if He has even more compassion and love for those who have been hurt by "Believers" who claim they are doing His work? He promises a significant return on what people suffer on His behalf – what is the cost of one's dignity and worth?

He promises the same reward (wage) to ALL those working on His vineyard, regardless of when they begin to work for Him. (Matthew Chapter 20) We need to feed all we meet with His Bread of Life and offer them a drink of His living water for we never know when we may be entertaining one of the Lord's own angels.(Hebrews 13:2) We have been given all we need in His Son, Jesus, and the Holy Spirit is the down payment on our inheritance as sons and daughters of Father God. What are we choosing to spend/invest our inheritance (talents) on?

The Wisdom of the Harvest

Wisdom waits at the Gate
Are you going to invite her in
Or will you wait?

Before the foundation of the world, Jesus was with the Father. Everything was gathered and the Holy Spirit was brooding, just waiting for the Father's Word to go forth. Wisdom was present at the foundation of the world as well (Proverbs 8:22-23). The intriguing thing is that by all appearances there was nothing... *"the earth was without form and void"* (Genesis 1:2), yet all three members of the Godhead saw the possibilities because they had wisdom! Had we been there, we might have simply turned away because there was nothing readily apparent for us to see.

The astounding promise of God is that: No eye has seen, nor ear heard, nor the heart of man imagined what it is that God has prepared for those who love Him (1 Corinthians 2:9). We need to remember to keep our eyes on Jesus just as He always kept His eyes on the Father to see what He was doing and what He saw. For it is *"the glory of God to conceal a matter, but the glory of kings is to search out a matter"* and the Kingdom of God is like a man who finds a treasure within a field and he hides it and then for *"joy over it he goes and sells all that he has and buys that field"* (Matthew 13:44). Father God sent His precious Son to buy back (or redeem) the world and all the treasures (his children) that were stuck in the world. As His sons and daughters, we are destined to rule and reign with Him as a Royal Priesthood, and as such we need to be looking for those who are still stuck in the world so that we can call out the treasure within them *"for we have this treasure in earthen vessels"* (2 Corinthians 4:7).

I believe that we are still in the final stages of preparing for the Billion Soul Harvest. For years we have been praying in the laborers to help with this Harvest, and I believe that this is the time for us to go to the Highways and Byways to search out the ones He highlights to us as they need to be set free from where they have been stuck so that they can begin to be transformed by the renewing of their minds. We need to begin training and equipping them (also known as discipling them) to represent the fullness of Jesus to the ones who will be coming in as the Lord's Harvest comes forth.

Glorious fields of gold
Are overlain with purest white.
The earth still holds
Numerous treasures of a sort,
Inviting us to dig in deep,
Unearthing Heaven's splendor
For a time such as this.
You never know what you'll find
When at first you enter in.
Sometimes it's easy to pull forth
Other times, an uphill struggle.
One thing is for certain though –
The adventure never gets old
When we watch the Father's Plan unfold!

We need to remember that Jesus paid the price to redeem everyone over two thousand years ago. It is our privilege to share the Good News with those who have not yet heard about or received what He did for them. We need to share it in a way that draws them to Him. What better way than sharing our Joy of the Lord with them as we encourage them? We can let them know that no matter what their circumstances are or how far they feel they are away from Him, He is right there. He is always simply waiting for them to turn and see Him, waiting with His arms wide open to receive them. Once they receive Him and invite them into their hearts, they have a clean slate. They are born again and all things are made new. It is then that the masterpiece of their lives can begin to come forth from the hand of the Master.

I Am
Putting on your new canvas cloth.
Everything has been erased –
Freshly made white,
A brand new start.
You are the Master Painter,
Etching the scenes of my life
Captured in living color
As you expand my heart!

We need to always remember to keep our eyes on Jesus and what it is that the Lord wants to do within each situation. It is never about circumstances, those are in reality distractions from the enemy, merely designed to draw our focus from the Father and His Kingdom. Instead we should be continuously asking Him how we can partner with Him to bring His Kingdom forth, asking Him to see things through His eyes and with His heart.

The fingers of your Love
Stretch out from afar,
Drawing us ever closer
To your heart.
Each day is a gift –
A present to be unwrapped.
What will we do with it?
Once we begin to walk with you
We are no longer the same.
The delight of our new lives
changes us from within
Until your abundant Love overflows.
Echoes of You in my heart
No matter where I go,
You free the flow
Of Peace, Love and Mercy,
Guiding compassion
To leave its mark
On heart after heart!

We need to set aside our opinions and look beneath the surface of those we meet to see the treasure that the Lord has placed within each of His children, especially those who do not yet have a personal relationship with Him. I believe that He is in the process of hedging His wayward ones in that they will return to their first love for they were with Him before the foundation of the world (Ephesians 1:4), and His Love Never Fails!!!

Partnering with The Trinity

Lord,
We take our Delight in you. We long to partner with you for your will to be done on Earth as it is in Heaven. We stand in the gap for those who do not yet know you and we are filled with joy because you grant the desires of their hearts to those who take their delight in you, and answered prayer brings fullness of joy. So we are full of the Joy of the Lord, confident that our prayers are arising to you as a sweet savor.

No one knows the hour of the return of your Son, Jesus Christ of Nazareth, but we look to that moment and as we see everything going on in the world today, it seems that these are the "last days". We want to partner with you to hasten the day of the return of your Son, Jesus Christ of Nazareth, so He may receive the fullness of the reward for His suffering. We ask in the mighty Name of Jesus that you would pour out your Spirit in a mighty way; pour it out on ALL flesh!

We ask for more of your Spirit so that the hearts of those who do not yet know you will be prepared to receive your powerful, life changing, transformational Love for we know that what the world needs now is Love - your agape, unconditional Love. For is only by knowing - becoming intimately familiar with and experiencing the depths of your Love - that we actually come alive. Your Love never fails. We ask that you would pour out of your

Spirit so that the hearts of the fathers and the hearts of the mothers would return to their sons and daughters. We need your Spirit - we long for you. For the Spirit and the Bride say "come".

Lord, we ask that you would help us to pray unceasingly for those who do not know you yet, for those who do not yet know your Son's great Love for them- His extravagant Love that was poured out for each one of us while He was on the Cross. In the Mighty Name of Jesus we pray, Amen.

Looking Through Kingdom Lenses

The following sections are some of the new ways of considering things that the Lord shared with me as I allowed Him to transform my mind from being of this world to being Kingdom minded.

Picking Up Your Cross

I was driving along one day, listening to the radio and the lyrics of the song drew me in. The song talked about how when we look to our circumstances in life, we will never see a true reflection of God's Love for us but when we look at the Cross that is where we will always see His Love poured out. All of the sudden my mind did a hop, skip, and a jump and I thought, "yes, I will always see how much God loved me when I look at the Cross!" What if in the Bible when it tells us to *"pick up our Cross"* (Matthew 16:24, Luke 9:23) it wasn't meant to be a bad thing, but instead it was meant to be a reminder for us to go back to that moment when we first discovered how much Jesus loved us and wrap ourselves in that Love and then head out each day? When we're wrapped in the Love of Jesus, then people will know us by our Love!

Entering in to His Rest

I believe that Father God wants us to get to know Him through and through. I believe that He is all about intimacy because He is a relational God. He never gave up on having a relationship with man, in fact He so strongly desired that that He was willing to sacrifice His own Son in order to make a way that we could enter back into relationship with Him through His Son, Jesus Christ. I believe that when the Bible talks about us entering into the "rest" of God (Hebrews 4:3) there's the possibility for a play on words. Consider Father God as the God of the Universe. The Bible tells us that the Earth is His footstool. The Bible also tells us that He birthed the Universe and usually when someone births something, they are bigger than what it is they give birth to. Here's where it gets tricky: the Universe is ever-expanding. What does that tell us about God? Maybe there's always the chance for us to learn a whole new level of God and enter in to a whole new depth of intimacy with Him. The Bible actually says that *"deep calls out to deep"* (Psalm 42:7). I believe this is an invitation from Father God for us to seek out the "deeper" things of God, those things we've not yet experienced. I believe that when we consider Father God as an iceberg, we've only seen the tip of the iceberg with God. We've only just barely begun to scratch the surface in our encounters with Him. When He invites us to enter into His rest, what if He is inviting us to explore the rest of Him, those things we've not yet experienced?

Hastening the Day

One day I was noodling with the Lord, just spending time with Him thinking and meditating on some of the scriptures that I don't fully understand yet. I was asking Him for greater understanding of some things and I came across the scripture in 2nd Peter that asks what sort of godly people should we be then, living lives of Holiness and godliness and working to hasten the day of the Lord's return (2 Peter 3:11-12)? My mind did a hop, skip, and a jump and I suddenly thought: what if by choosing to no longer relive the times when Satan was tormenting us, we could actually shorten Jesus' time on the Cross?

Please don't misunderstand! I am not establishing Doctrine here, I am just offering up an intriguing approach to living our lives as Christians. The Bible tells us that because Jesus overcame the world, we can overcome the world also. That means we are Overcomers. I believe that Jesus experienced every moment of my life that was anguishing, hurtful, or distressing to me while He was on the Cross and I believe He also experienced being accused of doing all those wrong things that I did as well. What if I actively choose today to never again relive those anguishing moments and in doing that it shortens His time of living through them on the Cross? After all, God holds time in His hands and He operates completely within the Supernatural Realm.

If nothing else, this is a really effective strategy to help people jump forward from being continuously harassed by the enemy through choosing to relive horrific moments in their lives over and over again if only through insisting upon telling others about those bad moments. If something happened to us once and it was horrible, why would we choose to relive it ad infinitum if there's a way to not do that? Let's just give it to Jesus because He paid for it already on the Cross. Let's step into our lives as Victorious Christians, being transformed from Glory to Glory, and never again merely be a victim.

Binding and Loosing

For a long time now I have been noodling on why the scripture concerning binding and loosing is phrased the way it is written. The Bible tells us that *"that which we bind on Earth will be bound in Heaven and that which we loose on Earth will be loosed in Heaven"* (Matthew 18:18). That has always confused me because it would seem to make better sense to me that that which is bound in

Heaven should be bound on Earth. In other words, it makes better sense to me that the direction would be coming from Heaven to Earth because after all, the Lord tells us in the Bible to pray for His will on Earth as it is in Heaven. Well, as I was noodling on this one day, suddenly I found myself thinking: well, what if when I choose to release forgiveness to someone on Earth that sets them free in Heaven to receive what it is they need Spiritually so that they can become who it is that God wants them to be on Earth? Wow, that's an awesome concept!

Once again this is not Doctrine! I am not trying to establish a new Christian Tenet, just merely trying to learn how the Lord sees things and wrap my mind around Kingdom Concepts. The interesting thing is that since having that thought, I've actually spoken to two friends who had fathers who had passed from their lives on this Earth before they had a chance to reconcile with them. Each of these friends had a subsequent encounter during worship where they saw their own father in Heaven and had spoken with their father during the encounter, forgiving him. In both cases, the father then walked away through a door leading to a different area of Heaven. Interesting. Like I said, I am not establishing Doctrine. I am simply proposing that maybe when we choose to forgive someone, it releases them spiritually so that they are in a much better position to receive what it is that they are in need of. I know for sure that it frees us from a Spiritual prison because it tells us that in the Bible in the parable of the unforgiving servant (Matthew 18:21-35).

187

Healing is for Today

Just as you may know many things I am unaware of because of your life's work and experiences, there are things I have seen in my experience as a minister on the streets. I have seen Father God heal a vast array of afflictions, ranging from simple but chronic pain (where the pure joy and wonderment on their face makes it clear that they are NOT just humoring you) to broken bones and specifically a shattered heel. Some of these miraculous healings were on foreign shores (Cambodia, India, Malawi and Brazil to name a few) where the people do not have access to Doctors and safe medical solutions, however many healings were also in the United States of America, in places ranging from Christian Conferences to House Church settings to the actual streets of the inner cities of Baltimore, Maryland and Columbus, Georgia. My point is that there are scientific facts such as a medical diagnosis, and then there is the Truth. His Name is Jesus (as you know) and the Bible tells us that all who approached Him for healing were embraced by His Grace. Their lives were transformed by His loving and compassionate touch; no one was told to go home and suffer, that it would "make them a better person". The Bible tells us that Jesus is the same today that He was yesterday and evermore shall be (Hebrews 13:5-9)! Good News! He wants to heal you!

Father God,

Your word says we have not because we ask not, so we are asking for you to touch our friend right now that they would know it is you in Jesus' Mighty Name. I thank you for your great love for them. I thank you for the plans you have for them...plans to prosper them and to give them hope of a future with you. In the mighty Name of Jesus, I command their body to come into alignment with the way in which you designed it to function. I bind up that Spirit of Affliction and I rip it out by the roots and send it straight to the Cross for Lord Jesus to deal with and I release the healing virtue of Jesus to every cell of their body to restore and refresh them from the top of their head all the way down to the soles of their feet in Jesus' Mighty Name. I thank you Lord for restoring the complete range of motion to them so they may walk out their destiny in you Lord. I give you all the glory Lord and I thank you for touching my friend in a tangible way with your everlasting love, in Jesus' Name I pray, Amen

Fasting and Prayer

What if the real idea behind Jesus' instruction for us to fast and pray was to cause us to spend time with the Father, learning who it is that He sees us as so that we would be better equipped to partner with Him and walk in the true authority that He has given us in Jesus' Name? After Jesus was baptized by John the Baptist and the

189

Holy Spirit landed upon Him in bodily form, the Holy Spirit then led Him out to the wilderness where Jesus fasted for 40 days as he was tempted by satan. I believe that Father God wants each of us to take the time to remove all the distractions of the world so that we can truly focus on Him. As we pray and spend time in His presence, uninterrupted by the world, we will begin to grasp the level of love that He has for us and His desire for us to co-labor with Him in order to advance His kingdom. I believe that He wants us to actively remove the unhealthy influences of the world so that we can then be filled up with His kingdom more and more and the fruits of His Holy Spirit would burst forth in a mighty way, letting the rest of the world know how changed we are once we invite Him in to our lives and our hearts to be our Lord and Savior. I believe fasting and prayer isn't meant to be a religious way of trying to work our way into the right position for God to answer a prayer, rather, I believe it's an opportunity to grow closer to Him and actually take the time as we pray to hear what He has to say and to learn His thoughts towards us and the situation or person we are lifting up to heaven. Fasting and prayer is an amazing Spiritual Weapon because it allows us to focus more clearly upon Him and bringing His kingdom to earth.

Let Jesus Change You

The fog is lifting
Ever so slowly,
Revealing details of the day.

Darkness is shifting
More and more quickly,
Opening hearts to pray.

Thoughts are changing
Bit by bit,
Taken captive to Jesus
For His final say.

It's never too late
To enter in through His gate,
Learning the ways of Love.

It's never too late
To allow yourself changed
By His mercy and Grace.

The only thing is
You must lay down your old life,
Rising up anew
To seek the beauty of His face.

Take a moment now
While He May still be found
And step straight in
To the Heart of Eternity.

Eternal Hope in Christ

Be Transformed

Diamonds in the stream of Life,
You alone, Lord, bring our hearts alive.
Thank you for the way you refine,
Cutting away the dead layer by layer,
Listening intently as we partner with you in prayer.
Dig deep, Lord!
Go after the things only you can find.
Help our hearts to align
As you get us ready for Harvest Time!

Eternal Hope in Christ

Leaning on My Own Understanding

In the mystery of a moment
My heart alights on you,
Simply standing there
Arms spread wide
And I feel myself begin
To come alive.

I spent my youth searching,
Always running in hot pursuit,
But never apprehending
The fullness of love
Readily available in you.

Now I'm diving deep ~
Wrapping myself in you
To be remade
By your heart for me.

No longer will I be
Unsettled and anxious,
Knowing
There is some part of me
Simply missing.

Instead, I'm whole!
For I am
Fully celebrated and loved
By the very one
Who stepped down from Heaven above
To pursue
Each and every one of us
With unconditional love.

Eternal Hope in Christ

Chapter 3: Strategic Warfare

Becoming Overcomers

The Bible tells us that *"they overcame by the blood of the lamb, the word of their testimony and not loving their lives unto death"* (Revelation 12:11). What does that mean? It means that because Jesus overcame the world and we are his, we have been given everything we need in order to overcome the world. The Bible tells us that in Him, we've been given every Spiritual Blessing (Ephesians 1:3) that we need in order to succeed. We've been given access to the mind of Christ, therefore we have the solutions of Heaven!

Jesus tells us that because the world hated Him (John 15:18) and we are no longer of this world once we belong to Him, the world is going to hate us too. We need to just get over it. We need to actually look on that as a great blessing because it lets us know that we are on the right track. We are headed towards victory. Jesus Himself overcame everything and then gave that victory to us that we would walk in victory, knowing that we are His. After all, we read the end of the book and we know how it ends, so we know who wins! We know we've been given everything we need in Jesus and therefore we are Overcomers also. The question then becomes "what is the word of our Testimony"? What is the evidence of Jesus in our lives? What is now changing that we ourselves could not change on our own? How is it that we can demonstrate the ultimate importance of having Jesus in our lives to the world? What is it that Father God wants to show the world through our lives? One answer to this last question is that I believe Father God wants to show the world His plan to help us all become who it is He always made us to be and who it is that He's had faith that we would become. Even when the world gives up on us, Father God never does. Probably because His Son paid such an extravagant price for our success!

The Transforming Power of The Word

One of the most amazing gifts that Jesus gives each Christian believer is the ability to actually finally become who it is that God always made them to be. Over the course of my life there were different times when I was not happy with the person I had become, but I didn't have any idea of how to go about changing myself. The beauty of the gift of Jesus and God's Love Letter to us as contained in the Holy Bible, is that when we take the scriptures that describe how God made us to be and how He sees us, and stand firm upon them, we can actually be transformed by them into who it is that He made us to be all along. I call this Scriptural Warfare and I believe that it is one of the most effective tools that any Christian has for overcoming the character deficits that used to just completely beset us and prevent us from changing our ways.

One great example of this was when I was trying to quit smoking cigarettes and my husband was still smoking two packs a day in my face. The only way that I was able to overcome it was by launching scripture at the thought that I might want to smoke a cigarette. For example, when that thought would come, I would declare out loud *"I can do all things through Christ Jesus who strengthens me"* (Philippians 4:13) or I would picture a cigarette and next to it I would picture Jesus and it was pretty clear who I would reach for.

Jesus says to follow Him. I believe that what He means is for us to follow the example that He gave us within the pages of the Bible. We need to take a look at how He overcame the world and then use His model so that we too can completely overcome the world and be transformed from Glory to Glory (2 Corinthians 3:18). One of the greatest ways to do this is to "mine" the Bible for effective scriptures that will help us to stand firm upon His promises. Scriptures like *"Christ in me is the hope of glory"* (Colossians 1:27) or *"greater is He who is in me than he who is in the world"* (1 John 4:4). Then, when you find yourself being harassed by satan (or tempted), you just declare that scripture out loud, as if you are launching a Scriptural Throwing Star right at satan's forehead! Almost makes it fun…

After Jesus was baptized, the Holy Spirit drove Him into the wilderness to Fast. At this point in time, Jesus was growing closer and closer and closer to Father God while worshipping Him in the wilderness. However, at the same

196

time, satan was doing whatever it was that he could in order to tempt Jesus. So during 40 days of Fasting, Jesus was being tempted all along! He never caved!! What He did instead was at the end of His Fast when satan came back to tempt Him again, He defeated satan by quoting scripture and reminding him, *"it is written..."* (Luke 4:4). The bottom line is, even satan knows scripture and he knows that it's the Truth and he knows that the Truth is what will set us free (John 8:32). Only the Truth will set us free! So we need to follow Jesus and use the vital resource that has been given us within the pages of the Holy Bible in order to fill up our personal arsenal with Scriptural Warheads that we can launch right at satan whenever he tries to tempt us. Remember, the Bible even tells us that when we are being tempted, God will always provide a way out (1 Corinthians 10:13). I believe that all we will ever need is contained within the pages of the Bible and that as we live our lives led by the Holy Spirit, we will know the ultimate loving relationship with Father God through Jesus!

Once we reconcile ourselves to the fact that the world is not going to like us, then we're able to move on to some of the greatest opportunities ever! We are able to allow Father God to use us to open the eyes of the blind. We're able to allow Father God to use us, those thought of as foolish, to confound those who think themselves to be wise (1 Corinthians 1:27). Over the course of the past year, Father God has been opening my eyes more and more to understanding that statement at a whole new level. I'm now understanding that He is using the foolish me who I know I am today, to confound who I thought I was back then (a pretty savvy person)! Only Father God has a sense of humor like that! I love His humor, don't you? All of Heaven echoes with the rumblings of the laughter coming forth from the throne room! The bottom line is, I figure if I can get God to have a good belly laugh then I'm doing something right. In reality though, I believe Him when He tells me in the Bible that He rejoices over me. I don't need to earn His rejoicing over me - that's just who He is!

Christian Divisions

If the worldly way is to always classify things, to identify things and put them into little categories so that we can better understand them, then Heaven's way is to embrace things. Heaven is not about division, rather Heaven is about unity and walking in unison while embracing all ends of the spectrum. As Christians, we have gone to great lengths to establish differences in Doctrine that then are turned into the foundational points for establishing different Denominations. All in all, this is simply division. God's not about division. God is about Jesus, and Jesus included everyone when He said *"Forgive them. They know not what they do."* (Luke 23:34) I believe that the time has come for us to focus on what it is that unifies us, and that would be Jesus. I believe that the very existence of all these different Denominations has become a point of sadness within God's heart. I believe that is time for us o let go of our differences and instead grab hands with he person next to us so that we can run together in unison, following Jesus! On a personal note, I love words and I love plays on Words. And when I take apart the word Denomination, it comes to mean "out from the name". So I believe that as we construct all these different Denominations, we are removing ourselves farther and farther out from and away from the Name of Jesus. Jesus was never about division, in fact He emphatically illustrated that concept to His disciples with the statement, *"if they're not against us then they're with us"* (Mark 9:38-41). So let's step up to the plate, and embrace the victory that Jesus won for us already and enforce it by tearing down all those things that keep us separated and instead focus on coming into Unity following Christ who is the head that we would all walk together as a functioning body, a body worthy of Christ's sacrifice on our behalf!

"If any man be in Christ, he is a new creation, all things are made new" (2 Corinthians 5:17)! This means that because of what Jesus did on the Cross, I don't have to receive anything less than what He accomplished for me. It means that I am an Overcomer. It means that I need to remember that God is the giver of all good gifts (James 1:17) and if something is attempting to latch on to me that is not a good gift I have the right to refuse it! When this happens and a Spirit of Infirmity or a Spirit of Affliction attempts to attach itself to me, what I need to do is **actively refuse to partner with it**!

One way to do this is to say "oh, thank you satan for reminding me to stand in the gap for other people who are afflicted by that Spirit because I know that because of Christ and what He accomplished on the Cross, I am not afflicted by that Spirit anymore". Then you pray and you intercede for other people who don't yet know the Lord the way you do, that they would be set free from Spirits of Affliction. You can even go to Jesus and thank Him for His promise that whatever the enemy tried to steal in the night would be returned sevenfold (Proverbs 6:31)! When you do that, you can then invite Jesus to go with you into the enemy camp and reveal Himself and His great Love for each person to seven people who've been afflicted with a Spirit of Infirmity, seven people who have been bound by the stronghold of Shame, seven people who have never known the Love of Jesus, and so on. When you have done that, you boldly declare: Thank you, Jesus, for the way You Love them! Thank you, Jesus, that they see you standing there and thank you, Jesus, that they have now been set free in the Name of Jesus. For he whom the Son sets free is free indeed (John 8:36)! Another thing that you can do is: at the next few Christian Gatherings that you go to, you can release a Word of Knowledge that God wants to heal someone who's suffering from a Spirit of Affliction or the Spirit of whatever it was that tried to latch on to you. This is another great way to advance God's Kingdom while undoing the works of the enemy!

Spiritual Reality

There is so much more going on within the Spiritual
Realm than we see at any particular moment in time. I
believe that we have an ever increasing opportunity to
see things in the Spiritual Realm if we only allow God to
help adjust our eyesight Spiritually. One of the things that
I believe we fall prey to is the suggestions of satan. I
believe that his Spirits of Darkness are continuously
swirling around us, suggesting that they are already in us
or upon us and just waiting for us to come into agreement
by saying "I have such and such". I really feel that it's
important for us to refuse to receive anything other than
what Jesus accomplished for us on the Cross. He was
victorious over Death on the Cross. He came that we
might have Life and Life more abundant (John 10:10)! He
came and then He conquered sin on the Cross and then
He went down into Hell took away the keys from satan
and then ascended back up to heaven where He sits at
the right hand of the Father (Mark 16:19). He told His
disciples that He had to leave so that His Father could
send us the greatest gift of all, the Holy Spirit (John 16:7).
We need to receive the Holy Spirit not any Spirit of
Darkness! We need to stand firm upon the fact that Jesus
conquered it all! He overcame the world and so can we
when we press into Him.

Spiritual Armor

God is so good that He doesn't simply issue one-size-fits-all Spiritual armor. In one regard, we all have the same armor (Ephesians Chapter 6), however on a totally different level, our armor is personalized by how we have experienced our lives as Christians. For example, if I walk in peace and I tend to not get ruffled or aggravated or frightened or anxious about things, then I have a greater comprehension of the peace beyond all understanding (Philippians 4:7) and the shoes of peace (Ephesians 6:15) that God has included in the armor for each Christian may be more well worn in my case; the peace component of my armor might look more polished than someone else's. If I have a greater understanding of Spiritual warfare, my shield (Ephesians 6:16) might look a lot more used and a lot more polished then the shield of another. If I am a person who struggles with coming fully into alignment with God's purpose and plan over my life, then when one would look at my Spiritual breastplate of righteousness (Ephesians 6:14), it may be clear that I need to grow a little bit in order to fully fit into that breastplate of righteousness. After all, we are all works in progress and ideally we are all progressing towards our goal which is to look more and more like Jesus each and every day. So on the one hand, we all receive the same components of Christian armor, but on the other hand each person's is tailored to them because God knows the walk that we each have before us and He knows the certain areas of our lives which are going to present a greater challenge to us, as well as the times we are going to need to really press into Him more than ever before!

As I consider that we are in the middle of a Spiritual war, I then need to take a look at whether or not there are any "chinks in my armor". One of the ways in which I can do this is to think across the span of my lifetime and take a look for patterns that continue to repeat themselves over and over again. To the best of my ability to explain it, circumstances typically belong to one of three categories. The first set of circumstances that we find ourselves in would actually be a consequence of a less-than-ideal choice on our part. The second set of circumstances would be an opportunity for me to establish a new level of Integrity within my character; this is the type of circumstance that can easily be spotted by situations which arise over and over again. When I look for those patterns in my life, what I'm really doing is seeing where I have fallen short of God's Plan in my life and looking to the Lord for the answer of how I can make it through that same set of circumstances and establish the Integrity that was missing before in my life.

Remember, back when I was living my life without having made Jesus the Lord of my life, satan was actually running me around the mountain over and over again. His way of doing things was evident in my life... In truth, it was a disaster. As soon as I realized that the only thing I was accomplishing was running my life straight into the ground, it was a really easy choice for me to invite Jesus in and ask Him to take over. Especially since He had already shown himself strong by delivering me from alcohol and my desire to drink at such an early age. God is so good that He actually even did that long before I was fully walking with him! We have no concept of the depth of His Grace until we truly examine our lives and see what are the things that He saved us from when we weren't even honoring Him! The final set of circumstances would actually be a situation that God knows that we will make it through and in allowing us to be tested on that front, He's actually offering us the opportunity to gain a whole new level of Spiritual Authority so we can then share our testimony of the way He delivered us and set someone else free in Jesus name!

Having explained all that, I want to emphasize that a "chink in my armor" is not a deficiency on God's part, but rather, it's an area that I still need to overcome in order to step into the fullness of Jesus' Victory on the Cross on my behalf. I need to enforce what Jesus already accomplished and take a stand proclaiming that "it is finished" within my life. In addition to those chinks in my own personal Spiritual armor, there are different things that I may have done during the course of my life that have opened me up to attack by the enemy by choosing to open one of the four doors of legal attack by satan. This would be a similar concept to the idea of opening Pandora's Box... . In short, the lid never fits back on properly.

The Four Doors of Legal Attack

There are different things which we can do, whether we realize it or not, that will open us up to harassment and attack by satan. In the most obvious case, when we continue to participate in activities which we know lead to death, or are sin, satan is well within his "legal rights" to completely attack us and our lives and our friends and family. In more subtle instances, there are activities that we can participate in and not even realize we are opening the door to allow satan into our lives. Examples of these come in four general categories: Fear, Anger, Sexual Promiscuity, and the Occult. I'm not going to go into extreme detail within these categories; my intent is to simply give an overview of the four doors of legal attack. There are many other books concerning these topics where you can find whatever level of detail you need.

The first area comes under the category of fear. Did you know that within the Bible it specifically says "fear not" 366 times? That is a "fear not" reminder for every single day of the year including leap year. It must be important to "fear not"! I believe one of the reasons why the Lord wants to reassure us is because He knows that through fear, satan attacks people. One of satan's means of gaining authority is through fear and intimidation. He's always trying to cause us to be afraid of things because then we play straight into his hands. However, the Lord wants us to know that we can trust Him as the Lord of our lives. Once we've made Jesus the Lord of our lives, we are in His hands and we should feel safe. He has a plan to give us hope and a good future, a plan to prosper us (Jeremiah 29:11). Father God has always had a plan and it is a good plan and He simply wants us to trust in Him. He wants us through our free will to choose to trust in Him and believe in Him and to not be fearful. The Bible specifically tells us that *"it is impossible to please God without faith"* (Hebrews 11:6). The Bible also tells us that perfect Love casts out all fear.

The reason why anger opens a door for legal harassment by the enemy is that it is clearly not a Kingdom virtue. So many lives have been destroyed by anger and the deeds that have been done in the heat of anger. Jesus Himself said: *"if you are even so much as angry at someone you have as good as killed them"* (Matthew 5:21-22)! This tells us that anger is not something that God is pleased with. Another concept for us to consider is that in reality what right do we have to any anger? God has done everything to open the way for us to return to having a relationship with Him again and for us to walk in His kingdom virtues, for us to actually have the fruits of the spirit (Galatians 5:22-23) within our hearts. In short, He has done everything necessary for us to succeed. When the God of the Universe, Our Father who is in heaven, gave up His own Son to die an excruciating death on the Cross in order to open the way for us to have a relationship with Him again after we messed up, how could we possibly be angry about anything? I think once again it comes down to: do we trust God, do we see what He's done in our lives, and are we going to choose His way of leading our lives now that we're back in relationship with Him again? There is also something inherent in anger that suggests that our way of doing things or considering things is the right way so it is okay to get angry with others because we are right! This is pride and it simply is not the case!

The next area of activities that leads us into a vulnerable position with satan is through acts of sexual promiscuity. In the Bible it talks about how married couples knew one another. This is a reference to the intimacy which occurs when one opens oneself up through sexual intercourse with another person. When people become sexually involved, there is a soul-tie which is generated between the two people. Our problem is that over the years as a society, we have grown more and more relaxed about what's okay and what's not okay within the realm of sexuality. The spin-off of this is that people are being intimate with one another in a casual way. This opens us up to all sorts of spiritual devastation.

When you actually pause to think about it, it'll really open your eyes. For example, when a woman chooses to be intimate with a man and that man has already established many soul-ties from past intimacies, the woman is now connected to all of those people through the soul-tie that's developed during the course of intimacy. When we look at it that way, it gets extremely complicated very rapidly. God intended for one man and one woman to commit themselves to each other through the Marriage Covenant, a Blood Covenant, forever as long as they both should live. When we bend our knee to our social culture and don't consider the repercussions of our sexual activities, we open the door for satan to attack us in a huge way. Once again remember that the kingdom standard is much stricter than our standard, so my guess is that if we even just look at something that we are not supposed to, we could be opening ourselves up to attack. On that note, I do have a question: why is it that we're okay with watching a sexual scene in a movie that we would not be comfortable with watching while actually standing in the same room? Maybe we need to re-examine our standards. Just a thought.

Another way in which we may inadvertently cultivate an unhealthy Soul Tie to another person is when we expect them to fulfill a need within our lives that really should only be filled by God. In some cases, if we have not had a fulfilling relationship with our father or our mother (on Earth) we might be more prone towards seeking out Spiritual relationships with people whom we would consider to be Spiritual mothers and fathers. If we are "needy" in this area of our lives, the enemy can possibly use this against us by tempting us to be more inclined to place more trust in the guidance from these people then we do in our own ability to hear straight from Father God or the Holy Spirit or Jesus. In each instance of our lives, we should always be taking each and every thing that someone else shares with us back to the Godhead in order to find out what it is that we need to know and what is Truth. When we place an expectation on another person to fulfill a need within our lives, we are setting ourselves up for a large disappointment potentially, as well as opening ourselves to attack by the enemy because we were placing greater trust in a human being than we are in God.

The area of the Occult actually encompasses a lot of different things. I'm not going to go into extreme detail here either, however, I will discuss some of them. The most obvious area would be witchcraft. I think it's pretty clear why that opens one up to the attacks of satan, however in a nutshell, it's because one is using his (satan's) power to gain what they want. Control and manipulation are included within the category of the Occult because, generally speaking, witchcraft (the Occult) is using satan's power in order to control or manipulate events. Trying to foretell the future using horoscopes, tarot cards, runes and other such devices also comes under the Occult and this is because numerous times in the Bible it was made clear that God did not want His people consulting others concerning the future, rather He wanted them to come to Him and to consult His prophets. Another way that the door to the Occult can be opened is through taking drugs or drinking alcohol to alter one's state of consciousness. Eventually the Spirit of Addiction grabs ahold of a person and their free will is compromised to the point of where their main pursuit in "life" is trying to regain that feeling of euphoria that they hope that the next drink or drug will bring them. One of the spin-off effects from this particular open door is that satan readily heaps shame upon a person who finds themselves addicted to substances. Shame is then used to isolate the person so that satan can really attack them, creating a never-ending cycle of horror within their life and the lives of those who love them.

Prayer to Close the Four Doors of Legal Attack by satan

Heavenly Father,
I thank you for your Son, Jesus Christ of Nazareth who died on the Cross for me. He is my Lord and Savior.

I renounce fear and refuse to partner with a Spirit of Fear. I send any fear I may have to the foot of the Cross for my Lord, Jesus Christ of Nazareth, to deal with for me.

I renounce anger and I refuse to partner with the Spirit of Anger. I send anger to the foot of the Cross for my Lord, Jesus Christ of Nazareth, to deal with for me.

I renounce sexual promiscuity. I will only be intimate with my wedded spouse or you, Lord Jesus. I send the spirit of lust and sexual promiscuity straight to the foot of the cross for Jesus Christ of Nazareth to deal with for me. I ask you to sever any unholy or unhealthy soul-ties in the Name of Jesus. I return to them whatever belongs to them and ask that those things which are mine would be returned to me, washed in the precious Blood of Jesus.

renounce the practice of control and manipulation and I refuse to participate in or practice occult activities or partner with any Spirit of Witchcraft, Control or Manipulation. I will not walk in rebellion. I send all the activities of the Occult to the foot of the Cross for my Lord, Jesus Christ of Nazareth to deal with for me. I choose to follow you and submit myself to your Lordship, Jesus.

I choose today to release forgiveness to any and every one who may have ever hurt or offended me whether they knew it or not. I release them to you Lord Jesus, knowing that you have a wonderful plan for their lives and I ask that you would bless them with a double portion of the blessings you have so freely given me.

Jesus, I give my heart and life to you as my Lord and Savior, and if there is any Spirit within me that is not of you, Lord Jesus, I ask that you would take it from me and set me free now.

HE WHOM THE SON SETS FREE IS FREE INDEED!

Lord Jesus, I ask that you would shut these four doors of legal harassment: the door of Fear, the door of Anger, the door of Sexual Promiscuity, and the door of the Occult and that you would seal them shut with your precious blood.

Jesus, is there anything else I need to address today?

(LISTEN FOR WHAT HE HAS TO SAY AND THEN
ADDRESS IT THROUGH YOUR OWN WORDS)

I thank you that I can do all things through you, Lord
Jesus, because you strengthen me, and it is in your Holy,
precious Name that I pray. AMEN.

All in all, God wants His Sons and Daughters to know
who they are and to know who He is. Numerous times in
the Bible it urges us to *"seek Him while He is near"* (Isaiah
55:6). It tells us *"when you seek me with all your heart
you will find me"* (Jeremiah 29:13). He invites us to enter
into "the rest" of Him, and I believe that this means He
wants us to come to know the areas of Him that we have
not yet experienced. He also wants us to rest, safely and
securely, knowing that He has our best interests at heart.
The Bible says that He wrote out all of our days long
before we were ever born (Psalm 139:16) on Earth and
He has a good plan. When will we learn to trust him?

Guarding Our Gateways

Once we become aware of the presence of the Doors of
Legal Access then we can be diligent in maintaining our
Spiritual Integrity by ensuring we always wear our
Spiritual Armor and by being extremely careful what we
allow in through our gateways. The Bible tells us to guard

our eyes and our heart (Proverbs 4:23) specifically. It also tells us that His sheep hear His voice (John 10:27). We need to steward that which we've been given which has now become his Temple (1 Corinthians 6:19-20) and we need to ensure that we take all thoughts captive and bring them to the obedience of Jesus (2 Corinthians 10:5). The Bible also tells us that because of Jesus, the gates of Hell won't Prevail against us (Matthew 16:18). For a long time I wondered what this meant and then I realized that if we are gateways releasing the Kingdom of God wherever we go, the people who don't yet know Jesus and belong to the enemy (even though they don't realize it) are releasing hell as they go. I'm not saying that people who don't know Jesus are demons, I am just saying that just as Jesus let the Pharisees know that they were "as their father was and their father was the liar of all lies" quite possibly the same holds true today.

It's quite clear that one of our main battlefields is actually our mind because of the way the world is continuously introducing thoughts and culture and ungodly opinions as well as non-Kingdom behavior into our consciousness. A good example of this happened during the 2012 London Olympic opening ceremonies. My good friend Lorraine and I were watching and were very excited for the beginning of the Olympics. Our excitement was short-lived though because it quickly became clear that there was a deep level of Darkness being released through the ceremony. At one point they had a nursery scene in which they had all these nannies dressed in gray come peeking over the bassinets of sleeping babies in a way that could only be described as threatening, or just straight-up evil. The next act was a famous singer who entered the stage riding on a huge giant black swan in a suggestive fashion. At that point Lorraine looked at me and I looked at her and we both agreed we needed to stop watching much to our disappointment. However, I think we were both glad that each of us had recognized the same thing. Since the Olympics are a worldwide event and each nation is curious about the customs and traditions of other nations, I believe the enemy uses this as an opportunity to negatively impact world culture in a way which is specifically designed to undermine the culture of the Kingdom of God.

Another thing that I noticed within the TV entertainment media realm is the incredible increase of medical advertising. Hand in hand with this, they now are required to read every single potential side effect of the pharmaceutical drug that they are pushing. It occurred to me that this is just another way for the enemy to release fear as well as potential physical maladies. What I mean by this is that somebody watching could very easily hear one of those side effects and think that they are having that "ping moment" of figuring out what's wrong with them and in so doing say "that's what I have!" The moment we come into agreement with and take ownership of a physical malady by saying "that's what I have", well then, that's what you get quite possibly. I believe that the power of life and death are in the tongue, therefore we need to always choose to agree with Life. When I go to the doctors and they give me some sort of a diagnosis of what they think is going on, I'm very careful how I phrase that to anyone. I specifically will only say "they believe that this is the case, however, I know that God is doing something far greater". I will not take ownership of a gift straight from Hell because my Father is the giver of ALL good gifts (James 1:17) and I don't have to receive anything less than what Jesus paid for on the Cross for me and that was complete healing. It may not have manifested just yet, but I know that I have a Good, Good Father and I know that He specializes in Miracles as well as Healing over time. I am simply a "work-in-progress" and I am looking forward to the day when the doctors see what God has done in me! Don't receive anything less and certainly don't agree with one of satan's slippery schemes.

Spiritual Atmospheres

At one point when I was receiving training for inner healing, I learned that is extremely important for us to be aware of our Spiritual atmosphere at all times. Shortly after being taught this, or told about this, as I was driving to a Worship Gathering and training event at the church that I was attending at the time, I suddenly found myself being angry and going over and over and over a conversation in my own head. I caught myself reliving what I should have said and what I wished I had said. Suddenly, I realized, "wait a minute that's not me. That might be who I used to be, but I'm not that person anymore. Because if any man be in Christ, he is a new creation and all things are made new (2 Corinthians 5:17)!

I then realized that I needed to make it clear that I knew that I was not that person anymore. So I declared it out loud: "I do not have a Spirit of Anger. I reject anger and I refuse to partner with an angry spirit. In the mighty Name of Jesus, I command you to go now, out that window right now, in Jesus' Name" and I actually opened the car window to allow the Spirit to leave, put the car window back up and then started praising Jesus. I then decided that maybe, just maybe, I was picking up on someone else's Spiritual atmosphere. So I decided that I should intercede for people who struggle with a Spirit of Anger and don't know the Lord yet. So I lifted them up to the Lord and I thanked the Lord that they were coming to know Him and that they would understand that He whom the Son sets free is free indeed (John 8:36).

Sevenfold Return Intercession

I then decided to "up my game" even more and I declared out loud "I stand firm upon your promise, Lord Jesus, of a sevenfold return for that which the enemy tried to steal in the night (Proverbs 6:31). Lord, you know I just apprehended the enemy trying to steal my peace, trying to steal my joy, trying to afflict me with a Spirit of Anger and so, Lord Jesus Christ of Nazareth, I ask that You would go with me right now, right into the heart of the enemy camp to show yourself to seven people who struggle with anger, to show yourself to seven people who have never had any joy, to show yourself to seven people who do not know your peace beyond all understanding. I ask, Lord Jesus, that they would all turn and see You and know that there is no condemnation in Christ (John 3:17) and that they would experience the shame that has been put upon them melting away. I ask, Jesus, that they would come to know you and they would receive what it is that you accomplished for them on the Cross so many years ago! For he whom the Son sets free is free indeed, so I declare freedom to the captives in Jesus Name."

After I finished declaring those things, I resolved that when I got to the Worship Gathering that I was on my way to, I would share a Word of Knowledge that Father God wanted to heal someone who struggles with anger and that's exactly what I did. After I gave the Word of Knowledge, seven different people came up to me asking for prayer to be set free from their struggle with a Spirit of Anger. Right then and there I knew that the Holy Spirit had given me an extremely effective tool for expanding the Kingdom of God while helping others to step into a new level of freedom! God is so good!

Learning About Spirits

Shortly after I arrived in Utah, I went to a gathering featuring a prophetic speaker. Even though I already had quite a few prophetic words which I still needed to step into in greater depth, I still went up to get a word. I think deep within there's always a desire for someone to "recognize the greatness that's just lurking beneath the surface within us", or maybe we just want affirmation that we're on the right track. In any event, the word that he gave me was that there was "a Spirit of Abuse" on me. That caught me off-guard! Where I come from that's not an encouraging word; I wouldn't call that something that edifies (Ephesians 4:12) one's standing within the Body of Christ. Apparently he saw the reaction on my face because he was quick to add: "No, no. You don't abuse others, there is a Spirit upon you that causes them to abuse you." Well, that was an eye-opener!

Basically what I got out of it was that, first and foremost, I believed that man heard from God. Secondarily I believe that if God told him that or showed that to him, God was taking care of it. So, all-in-all, I was quite relieved that I no longer had that issue! Later on when I considered some of the patterns in my life, I realized: you know, that guy may very well have hit the nail on the head. It's just something I had never given any thought to. My limited classification of demons was, as I already said, limited to demons who oppressed people and demons that possessed people; in both instances it was demons which caused people to behave in certain ways. I had never considered the fact that there apparently was a category of demons that cause people to behave towards us in certain ways in addition to those demons that cause people to behave in ways they don't want to behave.

This marked the beginning of me learning a whole lot more about the Spirits that satan will send after us or assign to us. There is and always has been a hierarchy within the Spiritual Realm. What if, just as there are Spirits that rule over geographic areas, there is a ruling Spirit assigned to our lives that has been with us all along and we are so familiar with it that we tend to be unaware if its presence and influence within our lives? What if instead of being set free bit by bit, we could be set free from the "Ruling Spirit" over our lives through Prophetic Deliverance and when it left, all lesser Spirits were also taken with it? Well, in order to be free from continual misinterpretation of my motives in life, I finally ended up traveling halfway across the country to attend a Prophetic Deliverance weekend during which I was personally set free to a whole new degree.

I learned that over the course of my life there had been a stronghold established by the enemy through fear and in order to counter the extreme presence of fear in my early childhood I had built a wall around my heart; although I built the wall to protect myself, it also prevented the Trinity from effectively reaching me. Since I was unable to receive the Love that I was craving because of my self-imposed wall, I went in search of it in all the wrong places. I became confused and thought that sexual intimacy was a reflection of Love, however that only really led me to shame. I also developed an angry spirit in order to be taken seriously as a woman in a man's world within the Military…heaven forbid that they think you were a "cupcake" in the Military as a female Officer. Over the course of my life, I had always gone to extreme lengths to develop and maintain friendships which was sometimes mistaken for "people pleasing". As I came back to the Lord and began walking ever closer with Him, I realized that I no longer wanted to conduct myself in those ways - Fear had melted away as I became established within my field of expertise. I had let go of anger and the need to try to intimidate others into respecting me, and instead was known as an Officer who would not order others to do what I had not done myself willingly already. I wanted others to do things I asked them to do because they respected me, rather than because they had to since I wore a certain collar device. By the time I was in my mid-thirties, I knew that every one deserved to be deeply loved for who they were, not for who they might become. After all, just because I might see a certain potential in someone, who is to say that they might not simply be happy as they were? In any event, I decided to wait for the one God had for me and not simply be in any casual relationship with someone just for the sake of not being alone. People are not made for our convenience - every single person on the face of the earth is truly a treasure and as such deserves to be respected and cherished. Unfortunately, after I met the one I thought God had for me, I learned that there was a whole new level of loneliness that one could experience despite being with another person 24/7. It was during some of those moments that I found myself thinking…"I will do this to show him, even if it kills me". Yes, I resorted to martyr tactics in the hopes of getting his attention to no avail; he already had enough going on in his own life that had spiraled out of control.

God is so good! He always always wants us to be increasing in our wholeness as well as healing our broken places and being set free. The very first time we acknowledge God and we say we found Him, He Loves us so much that He just lavishes His Love upon us right then and there, no matter our Spiritual condition. The best thing about God is that He Loves us so much that He doesn't want us to stay the way we were when we first found God (who by the way never really went missing... It was us who wandered off). The great news is that He kept pursuing me all the while and as I started going to Supernatural Christian Conferences, more and more of my "issues" melted away as the Father, Lord Jesus and Holy Spirit ministered to my broken heart. The challenge was that I still seemed to be misunderstood and my motives kept being called into question. I grasped the reality of the Biblical Truth that "out of the abundance of the heart the mouth speaks", however I still wanted to put an end to the false accusations, and the Prophetic Deliverance did just that! I was set free from a Ruling Spirit that has five distinguishable "faces" as well as reaches out to other Spirits, making a "False Reputation" about the person it is assigned to oppress; I was set free from the Spirit of Jezebel.

The Spirit of Jezebel has been completely misunderstood by the Body of Christ. I personally had no interest whatsoever in destroying any Ministry. It was far more

221

likely that the Spirit that was on me was trying to prevent God's Plan from coming together by blocking any ability I may have had to contribute effectively to others. From day one, I had no agenda - I was just trying to get through the day within the war zone of my childhood home. As I was growing up in a house without a Father, it was the seventies and the Police came to our house to warn us that Bobby Seale of the Black Panthers was going to be on trial and they anticipated rioting and we should sandbag our windows to protect ourselves. The following year, a young lady was raped in our front bushes. So there was more than enough fear to go around. I spent a lot of time trying to find friends to help me make my way through my isolated adolescence. I believe that satan and other demons specifically try to undermine and isolate us. These Spirits talk to each other and they twist the things we think we hear others saying to us within our conversations to get us off track. satan knows he cannot stop us from receiving our reward within the Kingdom of God, however, maybe just maybe he can get us off track or distracted and prevent us from being able to effectively testify to another about the goodness of God. The beauty of Prophetic Deliverance is that it is Spirit-Led and when the Ruling Spirit goes, all the rest must go also. After that, it is upon us to pursue wholeness by recalibrating our Kingdom Compass to the Truth as we replace the lies we had been considering to be true over the course of our lives from day one! In reality, that is exactly what God wants...He wants us to look more and more like His Son, Jesus, who is the Way, The Truth and the Life. It is only in Jesus that we can find the Truth which can then be

applied to our wounds to restore us to our created worth
so that we can fulfill our Divine Destiny in Christ.

Seeking Treasure

I long to see your goodness
Invading the depths of darkness.
Relentless light
Bursting forth from
The thickest of ashes.
A heart touched by mercy~
Drinking you in~
Living Water
Cascading down from heaven,
Awakening hearts once again!

Eternal Hope in Christ

Kingdom Treasure

Sparkling gems come to life
Once they receive the Light;
God's children start to shine
Once they've been refined,
Learning how to continue to dance
No matter their circumstance -
In all things we are to rejoice!
Not simply a suggestion - a command
Revealing God's perfect strategy and plan
For us to make it through this world's tragedies:
The louder our wilderness worship song,
The sooner we can move along,
Having the Lord redeem our circumstance.
As His Kingdom continues to advance,
The sooner we will see more clearly
What He wants to do through you and me.
He is relational, after all,
The One who restores us with Love after each fall.
It is all about Divine Adventure
For we were made for His good pleasure,
And each and every day
We look more like Him in every way.

Thank you Lord for your Son, Jesus-
The one who "died" so we could finally come alive!

Eternal Hope in Christ

Chapter 4: Harvesting Every Field

Kingdom Treasure

Whenever we go through something bad, the world's tendency is to run as fast as we can the minute we're done with it. To never look back. To just move on with our lives. In reality this is yet another attempt by the enemy to steal Kingdom treasure from us. I believe that each experience that we go through holds golden nuggets for us within it and what we need to do is ask the proper questions as we go through each set of circumstances. One of the best questions ever is: Lord what does this mean? Followed by the question: and what must I do?

The key is to turn every experience into an opportunity to receive what God holds for us because He's *"the giver of all good gifts"* (James 1:17) and *"He turns all things together for the good of those who love Him and are called according to His purposes"* (Romans 8:28). Well, we know that we were chosen *"in Him before the foundation of the world"* (Ephesians 1:4) and He called us forth for a *"time such as this"* (Esther 4:14) so when we look at that, we realize that every single thing we experience should be a blessing by Him, only the world gets in the way. So what we need to do is to learn to look on things from His perspective and see what is the treasure that He wants to give to us within that experience.

Harvesting That Field of Failure

While we cannot undo the past, Jesus can! The Bible tells us that if we confess our sin to the Father, He is faithful to forgive us and He will place our sin as far as the East is from the West (1 John 1:9). However, even knowing that, it is sometimes difficult to stop ourselves from being plagued with regret over failures in our lives. Basically the experiences in our lives can be categorized into good or bad experiences. One way to turn something that was considered to be bad into something good is to learn whatever we can from it. Within the world, it is a proven phenomenon that those who ignore history are doomed to repeat it. I know that I don't want to repeat any of my failures; I would much rather glean what nuggets of wisdom I can from them. I also know that the only way anyone can ever be blackmailed is by someone threatening to divulge something which has been held as a secret. So when I am faithful and I confess my failures, they are no longer a shameful secret which I can be blackmailed with by satan. I know that my past has been redeemed by Jesus and that since I now walk with Him as the Lord of my life, I have been given the authority to undo the works of satan in the Name of Jesus.

Jesus came to the world because Father God so loved the world that He did not want man to continue to be separated from Him for eternity due to sin (John 3:16). Father God also wanted the world to come back into alignment with the reason He made it; He wanted to redeem the world back to its created worth. Father God was confident that His Son Jesus was up to the task of redeeming the world from the curse of sin. In simple terms, Jesus told His disciples that His mission on Earth was to undo the works of satan. He also (much to our great delight) set in motion the pieces of the puzzle that allow us to choose to enter in to a loving relationship with our Heavenly Father, and to live our lives being transformed by the Glorious revelation of His love for us as we follow the promptings of the Holy Spirit on a daily basis. Through the gift of Jesus, we are able to enter into living Life more abundant (John 10:10), no longer merely struggling to survive. What a great time to be alive!

The Bible tells us that when the thief is apprehended in attempted act of thievery in the night there is a sevenfold repayment on that which he attempted to steal (Proverbs 6:31). Since we know that the enemy comes to steal, kill and destroy (John 10:10), and he is also the accuser of the brethren (Revelation 12:10), it is quite possible that satan played a role in some of our failures. Why not stand firm upon the Lord's promise of a sevenfold return when we apprehend the enemy in an attempt to steal our success? I believe that there is the possibility of redeeming the "Field of our Failure" by being willing to re-examine the lessons the past can offer us as we ask the Lord to show us seven nuggets of treasure that He has for us within those experiences which the enemy tried to steal from us.

The Bible tells us that the power of life and death is within the tongue (Proverbs 18:21). We can either choose to speak life or we can come into agreement with death. I choose life! I want to experience life and life more abundant! After all, that is what Jesus accomplished for me on the Cross and for you as well! Let's make sure that we get the full reward for His suffering so that we can glorify His name as we are transformed from glory to glory. Let's intentionally speak Life over others so that they too might receive a better understanding of their identity in Christ. Let's speak Life over others so that they might understand more fully the nature of the decision before them. Some of them have no idea that there's a Spiritual war going on all around them at all times. A lot of these people you and I might look at and think they already made their choice, and they are not choosing to be Christian or follow Jesus, however, I have learned that in an astounding number of instances, people have either never even heard of the Name of Jesus or they have no idea of how to go about making Him the Lord of their lives. That is devastating. That breaks Father God's heart. That comes down to us because we are the ones who know the good news and we know that we've been set free and we should be sharing the Gospel with anyone who will listen, even those who don't want to listen. We should be shouting it from the rooftops!

In the Bible, it specifically admonishes us that when we go in front of the judge we should not be anxious ahead of time about what we are going to say, but rather we should let the Holy Spirit speak through us (Luke 12:12). I believe hat God wants us to be led by the Spirit at all times! I believe that another way of looking at that particular scripture is that when we go in front of someone who is going to judge our words as to whether or not they are truth, we need to be led by the Spirit because it's only the Spirit that will convince anyone of anything.

believe that God does not want us to create a set way of doing things or a recipe for salvation or any sort of step by step process whereby we believe we will always achieve success. Rather, Father God wants us to trust Him and allow Him to flow through us because that's what captures someone's heart. When the God of the Universe speaks to you, it tends to grip you in a way that hearing from a mere man will not. So when we go out to share the good news of what it is that Jesus Christ has done for us, I believe that we should simply let the Spirit flow through us because the Spirit is the one who draws hearts to redemption (John 6:44). Instead of developing checklists and recipes for success, we should develop our ability to flow in the Spirit, as well as develop our ability to be led by the Spirit because His Love never fails!

Kingdom Harvests

The Bible tells us that the day will arrive when the sower will overtake the harvester: Behold, the days come, says the Lord, that the plowman shall overtake the reaper

(Amos 9:13). The question becomes: How will each react?

As Kingdom Christians, we need to begin to cultivate a respect and honor for the gifts of others. We need to realize that there is a time for all things (Ecclesiastes 3) and that there is a divine reason for each gifting. The Body of Christ has need for each and every gifting and ALL are needed for the Body to walk forward in unity.

Sometimes we can get caught up in thinking that we have invested in the preparation of the field and therefore we have ownership of the field. We may have sown seed in it, or spent time watering and nurturing the seed already present, in hopes of a good and plentiful harvest. In reality, Father God is the Master Gardener who tends the vineyards. He prunes what is necessary in order to control wild growth and to remove the things which take away from healthy growth. Jesus is the vine and we are the branches and we can only grow effectively when we are in Him, tended by Father God. Father God is the Master Gardener and He knows just what is needed to bring forth His harvest. The Lord tells us that He will give us fields we have not planted to harvest. *"I sent you to reap that for which you did not labor. Others have labored, and you have entered into their labor."* (John 4:38) Sometimes we are given the benefit of other's labors as we are sent in to reap the harvest of what we did not plant or cultivate.

It all comes down to the overall Plan that Father God has designed, for the Bible tells us that He has divinely ordained good works for us to do. *"For we are His workmanship, created in Christ Jesus for good works, which God prepared beforehand, that we should walk in them."* (Ephesians 2:10) It is His Plan and we should simply come into agreement with it. However, there is a human tendency to think we know better or that our way of doing things is wiser.

When the prodigal son returned and the Father embraced him, choosing to celebrate his return with a banquet, the elder brother who had stayed home to work his father's lands was angry. He felt shortchanged, over-worked and underpaid so to speak. His father asked him to celebrate with them, but he was angry and refused. He told his father, *"Look, these many years I have served you, and I never disobeyed your command, yet you never gave me a young goat, that I might celebrate with my friends."* (Luke 15:29) Apparently the elder son never felt celebrated as a son, rather, he felt he was merely a worker at his father's house. His father tried to reassure him, saying: *"Son, you are always with me, and all that is mine is yours."* (Luke 15:31)

I believe that we too sometimes become caught up in the doing and forget that the real reason God made man was for relationship, not to be a servant. I believe that we get busy doing ministry and that some of these ministries are not necessarily the works Father God created for us ahead of time, the works spoken of in Ephesians 2. Jesus warns us that there will be some who will not enter the kingdom:

> *Not everyone who says to me, 'Lord, Lord,' will enter the kingdom of heaven, but the one who does the will of my Father who is in heaven. On that day many will say to me, 'Lord, Lord, did we not prophesy in your name, and cast out demons in your name, and do mighty works in your name? And then will I declare to them, 'I never knew you'.*
> (Matthew 7:21-23)

Father God is far more concerned with whether we know Him than with what we can do in His name or on His behalf. We have a tendency to get caught up in the doing and in busy work, rather than choosing to spend time in His presence to actively seek His heart and partner with Him to bring forth His plans for advancing His Kingdom. Just as we are to know Him, He wants us to know each other for He is relational and He wants us to seek out the gifts in one another in order to call them forth for His kingdom. One of the most important jobs within the Body of Christ is to encourage each other as we do the Will of the Father. We are to edify one another always calling forth the good in one another as we pray unceasingly. We want His Will to be made manifest on earth as it is in Heaven.

Cambodia

Cambodia was my first mission trip. It was about 8 years after I began the process of coming back to the Lord, and three years after I became passionate for the Lord. We had a friend who had grown up in a children's home in Cambodia because there were already so many children in his family that they could not afford to care for him. Every few years he and his wife would return to Cambodia and the children's home in order to continue encouraging the children there to develop their art skills so that they would have a potential career path. On this particular trip, we were going to actually hold a conference on the supernatural to help one of his brothers who was a pastor. We were also going to travel to a village that had never seen white people and we were very excited about the possibility of winning their hearts to Jesus.

In order to get to the Village we had to travel two and a half hours by motorbike through the jungle. It was the wet season and there was lots of mud and standing water along the trails through the Jungle. Right before we got to the Village, there was a river that we were able to cross by loading one or at the most two motorbikes onto a Dugout canoe that was pulled hand over hand across the river to the other side by the woman who ran the ferry.

We had a great time in the village and made lots of friends as well as gave a package of rice and a water purifier to each person living in the village. On the second day we gave away a lot of clothes that we had brought for them and we also did face painting and just had fun with the people of the village. That whole morning we had been keeping an eye on the skies because it looked like a big storm was headed our way and we knew that the river was already running high and fast. We kept thanking Jesus for keeping the storm away.

We headed back to pack up our stuff to leave and when we got to the house on stilts where we had stayed, we discovered that they had prepared yet another meal for us. I'm going to be extremely honest here, I was not thrilled. I've never been super keen on rice, however my driver was benefiting because I kept handing him half of each plateful. My mind kept thinking "this is not good, the longer we stay here the more likely it is that the storm is going to hit and one of the people with us isn't even able to swim!" Well after listening to that garbage in my head for awhile, I suddenly realized that my friend from Cambodia probably only gets to see his family every three to five years and I needed to just celebrate his opportunity to see his family.

To make a long story short, while we were having lunch, the Village Chief arrived with a couple of the Village Elders. He told us that he "just wanted to see the white people one more time and to learn more about people who looked so different from him." As we interacted with him over the meal, the Holy Spirit took over and he ended up opening his heart to Jesus and his two Elders did as well and they all ended up getting baptized in the Holy Spirit!

It wasn't until later on that we learned that he was so transformed by Jesus that when it turned out one of our motorbikes was broken and we weren't going to have enough bikes to get us back to the city, he loaned his brand new bike to someone so that they could drive us the two and a half hours through the mud! When you understand that motorbike was his one big prized possession, and he loaned it to someone else to drive it through thick mud and standing water, then you realize just how profound of an effect introducing someone to Jesus can have!

The longer I have walked with the Lord, the more I have learned that the more I am willing to be inconvenienced on behalf of another, the greater the reward of Heaven! God is relational and he wants us to invest ourselves in each other! He wants us to be known by the way we love others. His Love never fails!

India

On my second mission trip, I was fortunate to go with a small team of people to India. While we were there we had all sorts of wonderful opportunities to interact with people as we shared our love of the Lord with them while preaching and teaching at various churches and small groups. One day we were to be the dignitaries at a church dedication ceremony, however we had not been able to check out of our hotel until much later than we needed to and because of that we were going to be extremely late arriving to the dedication ceremony.

As we were driving along in our vehicles we suddenly did a U turn, backtracked a bit, and then headed off the main road. We went to a small village which basically consisted of two cattle paths with houses built along both sides. We were told that there was a gathering in that Village to celebrate the death of one of the men of that village and we could see people arriving for the gathering on foot. After greeting the Elders of the village as well as the Widow of the man, we went to a spot along the path through the village and saw that the people had laid down all sorts of small burlap bags and pieces of material and that many people were already seated there waiting for us.

At this point in the trip, our photographer was running low on storage space on the SD cards she had brought with her to cover the entire trip and so I had been asked to take whatever photos I could as well as videos in order to capture some of the moments of our trip. As our leader started speaking, I happily headed out into the crowd to take pictures and was soon completely absorbed in my task. Before I knew it, I was completely enraptured with all the different colorful prints on all of the different articles of clothing and I was just taking as many pictures as I could of colorful patterns from India. Imagine my chagrin when I suddenly heard the Pastor say "Ede, would you like to come and give the Salvation call?"

Between you and me, I've never really been a closer; the kind of person who focuses on getting people to pray a prayer and receive Jesus, you know the one who closes the deal so to speak. Instead, I excel in planting as many seeds as possible by sprinkling scripture throughout every other sentence as I speak with people in foreign countries because I figure Father God can bring along someone to water those seeds - It's not my job. However when the Pastor invited me over, I heard myself say "Certainly! I would love to do that." As I got closer, he quietly said to me: "just make sure you transition well, you know, make sure that what you share is connected to what I just shared." Oh no! Remember? I just finished chronicling every single textural pattern available in the Indian garment repertoire; I had not focused on the entirety of the Pastor's message or to be completely honest, once I realized he was sharing his testimony I had pretty much tuned it out as I did what I thought I was there to do, taking pictures. So, my mind was racing, what could the possible link be? Oh I know, he shared a testimony therefore I'll share a testimony and that'll link it! Yes, that's what I'll do!

So I started off by saying, "Several years ago I found myself in a place where I didn't want to be; I was lost in the woods and I knew that I didn't want to be where I was, so the only thing that was available for me to do was to figure out how to get out of where I was. Well, when you're in the woods and you're lost, the wisest thing to do is to use a compass. However, if our compass is off by even just one degree, the longer we travel the more off course we get. Who here feels that your life is off track? Who here wants more of Jesus?"

To my amazement lots of hands shot up! Thank you Jesus for saving the day! So I led them in a very rudimentary "Salvation Prayer" and that was it! Later on as we were walking away from the village people kept asking me "Did you see all the people up on the rooftops?" Well, remember I'm the same girl who was out in the audience and got lost in the different beautiful patterns of India and so no, I didn't see people on the rooftops. As we continued walking away from the village, our Pastor noticed that the Pastor from India who was with us kept getting more and more and more excited. Our Pastor couldn't figure out why until he asked and the man explained that up until 15 minutes ago his congregation in that area consisted of five people and after what had just happened, his congregation had multiplied at least 6 times!

God is so good! On a side note, it was quite a few years before I confessed to my Pastor that I had no idea what he had preached about and he shared with me that he was a little bit confused by how I possibly thought that was a good transition. All in all, we laughed pretty hard about it!

In reality, the number of people who chose to give their lives to Jesus that day had nothing to do with me or even any of us. The Bible tells us that the Holy Spirit is the one who draws people's hearts to the Lord! That's why it's good news! It's not up to me to convince anyone - I simply have to present the truth and it's up to them what they choose to do with it.

My second big take away from my trip to India boils down to the concept that it's not about me and it never was. One of the things that I loved about this India trip was that our Pastor would randomly come up to us about half an hour before any one of our Gatherings and point to several different people and say "You, you and you are preaching!" Talk about having to rely on the Holy Spirit! However that's the best plan, because the Holy Spirit has a way of drawing people in that is Supernatural and it becomes clear that God is the one who's involved, not mere mortals or man.

Anyway, on this one day we were headed up to an area several hours away and we were going to have an open-air Crusade. After we had all gotten loaded on the bus and were traveling, our Pastor came back and pointed to

239

me and told me that I would be one of the people speaking. My brain started racing, and I could hear the little voices in my head saying over and over and over again: "I got nothing! I got nothing! I got nothing!"

The only thing that made any sense to say after that was "Well Lord, I need you to show up because these people want to hear something and I got nothing." Right about the same time that I was having this furious debate within my mind, my good friend seated across the aisle from me decided that it would be a really great time to share his entire life story with me... starting from let's say 3 seconds after birth!

So now not only did I have this amazing turmoil in my head but I also had someone else sharing their life story with me and was actually kind of expected to participate in the conversation. What a dilemma! Well the good news is I think I passed that Christian test, because I never once let on that maybe now wasn't the exact moment I would choose to hear his life story. And the best part is about 5 minutes before we pulled into town, that means three hours and 55 minutes into me beginning the great petitioning of heaven with "I've got nothing; Lord, you need to bring me something!", the Lord gave me probably one of the best teachings I've ever shared! So, He is always faithful! And He always has a plan! And as we honor others, He will honor us by always coming through for us, especially when we intend to share what He gives us with others!

Malawi

One of the things which became readily apparent while doing Ministry on the streets of the inner city in the United States, was that the key to actually effecting any kind of change or bringing hope to the Hopeless in a way in which it is receivable is to find someone within the neighborhood who is well-loved and respected already. Once the "Person of Peace" within a neighborhood is identified, it is then possible to come alongside of them and offer them help in the areas that **they** identify as being in need of the Lord's attention. In other words, as an outsider or someone who's known to not be from a given neighborhood, it's a challenge learning how to present an offer of help in a way that's receivable; you don't just want to come in making all sorts of suggestions for how they can change and improve their neighborhood. That doesn't go over well; not much is accomplished.

When we were preparing to go to Malawi and we knew that we were going to be going to smaller villages, the Lord impressed it upon us to pray to meet the Chiefs of the village. The same principle applies to small villages as does to the inner city or any established neighborhood - if you can find the "Person of Peace" who is already there and knows how things work and is respected, they can be the key to opening up an area that has not yet received the Lord.

Much of our planning and our prayers went towards asking the Holy Spirit to draw the hearts of the Village Chiefs to that point where they would be prepared to receive the Love of Jesus. We were praying that God would prepare the soil of their hearts so that they would be fertile and ready to receive the seeds that we hoped to plant so that they would bear a Great Harvest and much fruit of the Spirit. For some reason I felt as if my friend had much more invested in these prayers and so I suspected that she was going to be instrumental in touching the hearts of the Chiefs. I knew that God was going to show Himself strong for that Village that we were going to be going to along Lake Malawi in the Country of Malawi.

We traveled to Malawi with a group from Louisiana and the different people within the group each had a different Focus for their purpose for going to Malawi. One was an Architect who was going to help design a Conference Center for the people who had started this ministry in these Villages, and his wife was simply someone who knew how to love others well. Another person who went on the trip has a heart for the children who were being fed and going to the school which had developed over the years after the feeding program was inspired by one lady noticing one extremely hungry child and deciding to make porridge for that child. It's so wonderful how God uses small things to establish huge changes within a location as well as within a heart. The man who was leading our group married a woman from Malawi and through that had become family to the couple who had established the school and the feeding program along the shores of Lake Malawi. It was these people and their Ministry that we were coming alongside of in order to refresh them as well as help them extend the reach of their loving kindness to that village in an even greater way.

On our first morning in the village by the shores of Lake Malawi, we split up into teams and headed out to meet the villagers and just release the Love of the Father over those whom we met. My personal thought was that it would most likely be my friend who would encounter the Village Chief because I felt like she had prayed into it more than I had. You see I don't bombard Heaven daily with requests almost as if I'm begging, rather I pray when the Spirit of the Lord provokes me to pray and to be quite honest I hadn't really prayed too earnestly or even fervently about the Malawi trip, rather I was trusting God to work out all the fine details. So off we headed into the village.

The very first house we came to had a few people gathered round out front and so we went up and as I was speaking to them we saw a man walking jauntily along the path towards us. I turned because the Lord highlighted him and so I interacted with him and shared the word of knowledge that the Lord had given me about an ache or pain that he had in his leg. That opened the door for me to pray for him because, yes he did have that pain, and yes he gave me the authority to pray for him when I asked if I could pray a blessing over him. I was very particular and how I phrased it because I saw that he was wearing

243

what would appear to be a Muslim head covering and so I wanted to make it clear that I was honoring him and asking him for permission to pray. He gave me the permission and I immediately entered into praying a blessing over him by asking the Holy Spirit to touch him from the top of his head down to the bottoms of his toes. A huge smile swept across his face and he was very very enthusiastic and happy as he continued on his way along the path.

I turned back to the house and saw that a few more people had come up since I had turned and was talking with the man and so I returned to speak with the people on the porch who had gathered there. The Lord gave me another word of knowledge and so I asked the lady whose house it was if she had pain and she said yes she did, so I offered to pray. One thing that I noticed was that as I prayed for people my interpreter would not repeat what I was saying because they believe prayer is a sacred moment, so I boldly stepped into it and released what I heard Heaven declaring over each person I prayed for that day!

As we continued our travels through the village we encountered person after person after person and I would experience a brief sensation of pain or discomfort and based upon it I would ask them if they suffered from the same. Time and again they said yes! So I learned that sometimes the Lord speaks to us in subtle ways and instead of it being a big huge WOW moment, these pains were things that could have easily explained away by believing... "Well, of course your leg hurts, you were just hunkered down in the sand so of course it hurts when you stand up." What I learned that day though was that when I'm faithful and I go out on the limb for Jesus, He will always meet me right there and lavish His love on the one in front of me!

As we walked deeper into the Village, another man came walking along the path with a brisk step, and I got to word of knowledge for him so I went up to him and shared. He said yes he did have a problem with his knee and I asked if I could pray a blessing and he said yes and so I prayed that the Holy Spirit would meet him right there!. At about this time, my interpreter turned to me full of amazement and said "it's unbelievable - everything you say is true!" And I said "well I'm just hearing what the Father has to say and just sharing that with these people so of course it's true. He always speaks the truth and He loves each and every one of His sons and daughters!" What my interpreter said next absolutely floored me. He shared that the first man we met was the Chief and the third man we met was the Chief of Chiefs! Who knew?! Well, when God is in it, amazing things happen! We were off to a fine start!

As we traveled around, my goal was to train and equip the people who were walking with me as well as the people of the Village. I did not want anyone to think that I for some reason had a marvelous gift of healing or prophecy, but rather, I wanted to make the point that anyone who is a son or daughter of the most high God has access to Jesus at all times once they invite Him into their heart to be Lord of their life. As we continued on, whenever I would pray for someone to be healed based upon a word of knowledge, I would have one of the villagers put their hand on the person in need of prayer and I would have them repeat the prayer after me in order to let them know that it was not about the "Great White Hope" but rather it was about the God of the Universe who loves them with an everlasting love!

Another goal that I had was to help whoever was ministering with me become comfortable with operating in the gifts of words of knowledge as well as healing so when she was least expecting it, I would go up to someone within the Village and say "my sister has a word for you" and she would be caught off-guard for a moment but then she would share what God put on her heart for the person and it was always spot-on! She was very good-natured about the way I was activating her by just putting her on the spot. Sometimes it's best to be caught off guard so that we don't have time to allow doubt to creep in or fear to grip us. Especially when we are just learning.

As we made our way through the Village, we ended up coming upon a woman sitting near a tree all by herself. She seemed to be one of the Elders of the Village so I wanted to honor her and to visit with her. I asked her if she had pain in her legs and she said yes and so I spent some time with her and we prayed a blessing over her. The entire time that I was with her she was looking down at the ground and writing with her left hand in the sand. As I was interacting with her, I felt myself being pulled up into Heaven and I heard the Lord say "that what you do for the least of these you have done for me." I felt as if I was reliving a moment pulled straight out of the Bible while at the same time experiencing a moment with someone here on Earth. Very interesting experience to say the least! Soon it was time to return to our friends' compound in order to eat lunch so we made our way back through the Village waving to our new friends all the way.

When we arrived back at the compound after our morning out in the Village, our leader came up to me to let me know that there had been a lady whom he had met who was extremely sick and he wanted us to go after lunch to pray with her. He told me that she had HIV and was extremely depressed. My heart leapt within my chest because when I had been in India some of the members of our team had prayed for a woman with HIV and her family was so touched by the encounter that her son and husband give their hearts to Jesus right there on the spot. The woman herself was also touched directly by Jesus in such a dramatic way that when she went to her Church the next day, absolutely no one recognized her! She was glowing with health! So I knew that God wanted to do the same right there in Malawi.

Once we had eaten lunch, we headed towards the lady's house with a couple of other women in order to meet her and pray with her. We spent a good bit of time interacting with the woman who was clearly depressed and

247

saddened by her circumstances. I felt led to share with her concerning forgiveness and the freedom that offers the one who actually forgives and then led her through some prayers concerning forgiveness of her husband who had himself died from AIDS. I shared the testimony of the healing in India with her and then we prayed. By the end of our time with her, she was noticeably improved and much happier. As I closed our visit with her in prayer, I wanted to make sure that she knew that there was no shame in her sickness. I wanted her to know that I knew she had done nothing to deserve being sick and that I was not afraid or concerned that I might catch HIV from her. As I prayed, I heard myself thanking God for "giving me such a beautiful sister" and I then closed the prayer by giving her a huge hug and a kiss. We left and I was confident that the Lord had touched her in a significant way and I was eager to see how her healing would be made manifest on Earth as it is in Heaven.

The next day as we headed out into the village I experienced many dark thoughts. I felt like I had nothing to give anyone and I even felt like it had been a complete and total waste of money for me to even come on the trip. That's how satan attacks. He just surrounds us with dark thoughts and fortunately I've had enough training in Ministry that I knew that I was actually picking up on the atmosphere of the Village. I knew that these thoughts were not truth! I still didn't feel like I had much to contribute though, I have to admit. As I walked through the village with my team, I was at a bit of a loss for where to even begin so I just kept walking along thanking God in my heart for who He is and knowing that when I'm at my weakest, He can be His strongest through me. Suddenly I looked over to my right and I saw a woman at the Village well. And remembering my experience of the day before with the elderly lady underneath the tree, I thought *a woman at the well* what a great place to start! So I headed over to the well.

My interpreter begin a long conversation with the woman and I found myself just enjoying the day with my friend and the small tribe of children that was increasing moment by moment. Since the people of the Village had never really seen white people, we tended to generate a large crowd no matter where we went. Unfortunately the majority of the interactions that any of these villagers had with white people involved tourists and the Malawian people trying to get whatever they could from the tourists. So there was a bit of a Spirit of Entitlement over the area that would cause the children to say "Madame, give me bottle!" To be honest, by the end of my time in Malawi whenever I heard that phrase my skin just crawled and I have to confess I didn't have much love in my heart whenever I heard that phrase.

The challenge was that there was a growing crowd of children at this point and they were getting a little bit pushy. So my thought was: if I can just lay hands on these kids, then they would experience the Holy Spirit and maybe they'll settle down. So that's what I started doing! My friend saw what I was doing and she thought it was a good idea too, so we both started praying in the Spirit over the children. When our Interpreter finally wrapped up his conversation with the lady at the well, I asked him to ask the kids "who felt something when we were praying?" Many hands raised in the air. I explained that what they had felt was Jesus, and I then asked who would like to feel more of Jesus? Just about every hand was raised and the kids started jumping up and down. So I had our Interpreter direct them to repeat after me, and then I led them in the a prayer, inviting Jesus into their hearts to be their Lord and Savior and then asking the Holy Spirit to touch them from the top of their heads all the way down to the bottoms of their feet that they would know that the almighty God of the Universe had touched them. All in all, I think about 40 children give their hearts to the Lord that day which was awesome! God is so good! When we give our lives to Him, He always knows just what's needed for every situation!

Later that afternoon when we were back at the compound, someone came to get me saying that I had a visitor. I grabbed my friend in case the person needed prayer and we went out to see who it was. There was a woman who had a bit of a stomach problem and so I declared that my own body was experiencing a word of knowledge for her to be healed and prayed healing over both of us and was believing that we were both healed. It worked, because shortly after that I had to excuse myself as my body finally began working properly after our long travel to Malawi. After about 45 minutes of visiting with the woman, she made a comment about how she had really just wanted to see "her sister" and I suddenly realized "oh my goodness! This is the lady from yesterday!"

She was so transformed that none of us had even recognized that it was her! God is so good! A few minutes later she asked if it would be alright for her to go and get something to eat before the graduation ceremony for the children. I said of course and I apologized for having kept her for so long. Well, about half an hour later we went down to where the graduation ceremony was set to be staged and there was a row of chairs for dignitaries, the Chiefs, and for us, and plenty of seats on the ground for the children and the parents of the school.

Imagine my surprise when I looked over and saw the first two men whom I had met in the village, the Chief, and the Chief of Chiefs and sitting right between them was - my sister! Who would have ever guessed?! My sister whom the Lord healed from HIV and its complications was a Chief! Oh how I heard Heaven laughing!

It's when we know the least that God can do the most with us! If I had had any clue that first morning when I set out to the Village of what God's plan was, I would have been intimidated and I would have been convinced that I would mess it up somehow. All that was needed though was my obedience and my willingness to stop for and Love the one in front of me to the best of my ability. It's true we can do ALL things through Christ Jesus who strengthens us! The sooner we get to the end of ourselves, the sooner we can tap into the resources of Heaven!

Brasil

We went to one of the beachside towns in Brasil to explore during one afternoon. We wanted to get a screen protector for our friend's new phone. While we were there, we gave a Word of Encouragement to the man putting it on her phone. As we were leaving, one of the other young men came outside with us. My friend began speaking with him and he ended up doing a spontaneous Rap which she put on Facebook Live.

We walked down to the beach next and we saw a man with his right hand wrapped like it was broken. We asked if we could pray for him. He was happy for us to pray for him since he needed to be able to go back to work. We told him that he himself should lay his own hand on it and thank Jesus for healing it each morning. As we spoke with him, his wife got goosebumps! She looked amazed by what she was feeling. We continued on our way, looking for whoever the Lord was highlighting.

As we were walking along the street later on, a man on a motorcycle called out to us as he went past. I thought he was our Host, and turned to see the man turn his bike around and come up onto the sidewalk. He had a helmet on and spoke to our Brasilian friend, telling her: "the peace of The Lord" and continued on to say,"God is confirming the desire of your heart!"

The man was a complete stranger! Yet he heard The Lord and stopped to give us a Word. The desire of our friend's heart is to be a missionary. Our desire is to see others be empowered to walk out their Destinies and for people to be encouraged by knowing that The Lord loves them and believes in them, knowing they can overcome whatever is holding them back from their Destinies.

How wonderful to receive such a blessing while we were out on the streets to encourage others ourselves.

Last night, several children were baptized in the Holy Spirit and two chose to invite Jesus into their hearts, giving their lives to Him. Two women came up for prayer and had Encounters with The Lord, simply standing there with their eyes closed for about five minutes each. We celebrate what The Lord is doing!

When we returned from preaching at the Church, our hosts were having a chahascaria (BBQ) celebrating their father's Birthday. As we were talking with him, he was surprised at how much I could understand when they were talking in Portuguese among themselves. I explained that I had studied Spanish in High School many years ago. He said that he was not good at languages because Castilian Spanish is spoken too fast and Guatemalan Spanish is slower, but since he lost his hearing in one ear, it was too hard for him to understand. When I heard that, I knew we needed to pray for him.

We prayed and his ear opened!!! We prayed two more times and you should have seen his face when he realized that he could hear other people talking at the far end of the porch! The Lord gave him the best Birthday present ever!!! The next morning we heard from our hosts that his hearing was so improved that the sound of the ceiling fan had actually woken him up!

A couple of days later, I began to have significant pain on the left side of my back. I was having trouble standing up fully and it was extremely difficult getting into and out of the back seat of the car. I began to actually wonder whether I might have a kidney stone or something else going on, the pain was so attention getting. Finally I set my sights on Heaven and decided to refuse to receive this pain into my life and instead started giving a word of knowledge to every person I ran into concerning debilitating back pain. I turned my focus to Jesus and what He might be doing (word of knowledge for healing), rather than looking on my apparent circumstances (significant back pain). The next afternoon our hosts took us to meet their other father. When he got up to greet us I immediately asked whether he had significant back pain? He did! We prayed and he was healed and then we learned that he had been diagnosed with Parkinson's so we prayed to break off all generational curses, all word curses and to Divinely edit his brain activity by re-establishing the nerve pathways so they would effectively transmit signals and he could regain full mobility. He immediately began weeping as the Lord touched him in a significant way. We learned the next day that all the symptoms of Parkinson's had gone! Jesus is just that good and He loves each and every one of us with an everlasting Love!

The more we minister, the more we realize we are here for one on one encounters rather than for "Church". God is all about relationships! He really is pouring out on His Sons and Daughters. He really is looking for the hungry ones; the ones who were pushed away by the Spirit of Religion. He wants them to know who He really is and that His heart is for them!!! He wants each and every one of His Sons and Daughters at His Wedding Banquet (Matthew 22:9)! How can they be there if they have not been invited by us? We have an incredible opportunity to invite to prodigals (Luke 15:11-32) to come home. We can be those who are known for the way we Love (John 13:35). We can be instruments of reconciliation, His Ambassadors (2 Corinthians 5:11), inviting the lost, the last, and the least to enter in to His Kingdom!!!

WHAT ARE WE WAITING FOR??!

Hidden Treasure

A sea of light
In the depths of darkness,
Revealed by night,
God's harvest is ready.
It is far beyond ripe!

His desires in their hearts
Pull out our light in the midst of darkness.
Seeking out the very truth
Which will set them free
From those very same things
That used to plague you and me.

God's truth will prevail,
Penetrating deeply into hearts
Far and wide,
Acting like a spiritual bombshell
Decimating decades of lies.
Setting captives free.
Revealing God's heart in both you and me.

Kingdom treasure abounds,
Sprinkled liberally on the ground,
That safe field which Lord Jesus bought
By hanging upon the cross.

It's time to gather up
The prize for which He paid-
All those souls He alone has saved.

Eternal Hope in Christ

Harvest

All the earth worships you
Singing praises true
All in a delicate harmony
Balanced through and through

Spirit to Spirit,
Hearts in agreement.
All because of you,
Holding us together,
Yet allowing creative differences.
Each one made purposefully
To reflect a unique aspect of you~
Without each and every one,
The masterpiece is incomplete.

And so we search-
Going to the hidden places
As we seek you out
In every single face.
Delicate and true,
Full of weakness without you.
For it is you alone who came bringing life:
Equanimity in the midst of strife.
And you alone gift us with peace,
Saying "Bring me your burdens".
You alone take our load,
Inviting rest
While setting us free to become our best!

Eternal Hope in Christ

Endtime Leaders

Grace pours down
On an upturned face.
Hearts expand
As freedom hits the mark
And one after another after another
Arises, stepping into their place.

We have an army of spiritual giants,
Standing steadfast on your promises,
Knowing they were born for this-
Their finest hour.
They have counted the cost
And consider nothing lost
Now that they know your great Love.

In the end, it's what gets us through,
Experiencing your great Love
As we are refined by you.
Hand-picked from the ashes of what we once knew
Only to encounter the depths of you.

It's all in the knowing,
The deep solitary intimacy
Where we learn to trust,
No matter what.
Knowing, just knowing
The Goodness that is you.
Glorious, Magnificent, Wonderful and True,
We find all our Joy within you,
Wrapped peacefully in your great Grace!

Eternal Hope in Christ

Chapter 5: Emperor for a Day

ntroduction

This Chapter contains a variety of Lessons Learned which don't seem to fit in any other Chapter. I believe that God s always training us to step into ever-increasing levels of authority. I believe that in the course of that training, we earn things as we experience the worldly way of doing things and we discover in some instances just how unpleasant the world's way of doing things can be. These Lessons Learned can be instrumental in helping us to step into a new level of honor and can also teach us a lot about treating others as we would truly rather be treated ourselves (Matthew 7:12). I choose to take a closer look at all the unpleasant situations that I encounter during my Christian walk by considering them to be fields ripe for harvest. I believe that in each field there is treasure of incredible value to God's Kingdom. No matter how distasteful it was when I walked through that field of experience the first time, I am willing to go back and stand firm upon God's promise that when satan tries to steal things in the night, there is a sevenfold return. So I return to that experience and I partner with God by asking Him: "what are the seven nuggets of gold that You have for me to learn out of this whole experience?" These are Lessons in leadership and integrity, and Lessons in just straight-upright human decency.

259

Having been on the receiving end of some less-than-ideal Christian exchanges, I understand that not every encounter with fellow Christians is an uplifting one. In order to focus on the good that God has within these painful scenarios, I have created a file in my mind that I have named "When I am Emperor for a Day". The point is, I believe that God keeps His promises; He is not a man that He could lie (Numbers 23:19). I believe that He meant it when He told us in the Bible that there is *"a sevenfold return for that which the enemy is caught trying to steal in the night"* (Proverbs 6:31) and so, for that reason, I am willing to revisit these situations in order to glean from them the nuggets of wisdom that God has for me. I don't want to "do unto others" as I have experienced through negative situations, rather, I want to learn what God has in the midst of those situations because I truly do believe that for everything satan comes to steal, kill, and destroy, God has greater for us... He is just that good!

I would far rather consider how someone else might experience my treatment of them than risk hurting someone or turning them away from what it is that God has for them. In short, I would rather err on the side of caution, and so doing, learn Heaven's approach. Remember, our words bring either life or death (Proverbs 18:21). So it's imperative to consider the possible effects of what our words are going to be releasing before we just randomly release things here and there. The Bible even warns us that we're going to be held accountable for every single idle word (Matthew 12:36)! That takes things up to a whole new level, as Jesus always does. (Have

260

you noticed that?) For instance, Jesus talks to the disciples and He tells them, "listen, if you've ever even just been angry with someone, you have as good as murdered them in My Father's eyes." WHAT?! That puts a whole new spin on things!

Know Your People

As a Leader, one of the most important things you can do is to get to know the people you are running with. Learn what their strengths are. Learn what their hopes are and what their dreams are. Learn what it is that God seems to have made them to do, and then do whatever you can to equip them and encourage them in those areas! Speak Life to those dreams! Fan the flames of their spiritual desire! Encourage them to go after Him for all they are worth. Train them to **always take every thing** back to God so that they hear from Him what He wants them to know!

When I consider the question of Isaac and Abraham, I believe that basically what it boiled down to was: God wanted to know that Abraham chose God over the human desire of his lifetime which was having a son. When we take a good, hard look at our lives and some of the tests that we have faced, they come down to that same big question of: do we want God more than anything else? I have to say that based upon what Jesus endured for the "joy" of having our company for eternity, I think God is far within His rights to press the issue with us by asking us to consider what lengths will we go to for Him?

Please don't misunderstand me. God never sets out to destroy us or hurt us. He doesn't have to, satan is pretty well focused on doing those things. Have you ever wondered how it is that satan can get to you so effectively? Just a thought: it might be because you belonged to him before you joined God's Team. Unfortunately, satan knows what our weak areas are and he knows what's worked in the past and he just goes back to those same hurts and bruises and thumps them over and over and over again, hoping something will take. The only way to effectively stop satan is through launching what I call "Scriptural Warheads" at his forehead. He knows the Scripture - he probably knows the Bible even better than some of us do, and he knows when he's defeated. He knows that the Scripture actually reads: *"submit yourself to the Lord, resist the devil and he must flee."* (James 4:7) Our biggest problem is most of us haven't submitted ourselves to God. We just think that if we resist the devil, he has to flee. Not the case my friend. Yet another strong argument for making Jesus the Lord of your life and submitting to Him and His Lordship. For when we make Jesus the Lord of our lives and He's in us and we are in Him, Father God hides us in Jesus and when we stay hidden in Christ, we are protected. Sometimes God will keep pressing the issue by asking us if we're willing to give things up and as soon as we get to the point where we finally say "yes, I am willing to do it Lord! I will submit to you! Whatever it is you want, Lord!"

Boom! He makes a way and we don't have to do that final sacrifice; kind of like Abraham finding the ram tangled in the bush that he was then able to sacrifice instead of having to sacrifice his own son, Isaac.

There's so much that God wants to do for each one of us. One of the greatest challenges is that He is a gentleman and He will always respect our free will; He will not operate outside of the confines of what we will let Him do. So, if you have put God in a box, don't you think it might be a good time to take Him out of that box by asking Him: "Lord what is it that You want to do for me in this situation and who is it that You want to be for me in this situation?" That way you are letting Him know that you are trusting Him with the situation, fully confident that He has a Plan!

Defeating the Enemy's Strategies

We need to always remember that satan is very familiar or even "well-versed" on the scriptures. (Pun intended). He knows all of the scriptures because he was in Heaven as a key Angel before he succumbed to pride and fell like lightning (Luke 10:18). satan knows that a three-strand cord is next to impossible to unravel and for that reason, he has developed his own three-strand cords to tie us down and prevent or slow down our Christian progress. One of these three-strand cords is a twist on the idea of strength in numbers. The Bible tells us that it is better for two then it is for one because if one falls down, the other can help him up (Ecclesiastes 4:9). The Bible also tells us the three-strand cord cannot easily be broken (Ecclesiastes 4:12). satan's twist on this is that he knows that if he can send several different people with accusations or incorrect portrayals of a Christian, the likelihood is that the person hearing those reports will believe it because of the world's theory of strength in numbers. For whatever reason, we are much more inclined to believe something if numerous people bring similar accusations.

It's important for us to take a look at Biblical truth in this instance. When Jesus was actually being lied about by the Pharisees and the crowd chose to crucify Him (Matthew 27, John 18:28-40), it was based upon multiple reports concerning Him that simply were not true. So if satan would use that strategy against Jesus, why wouldn't he use it against us?

One of the greatest challenges for people who are in leadership positions can occur upon receiving bad reports about another person. After all, if we are truly Kingdom-Minded Christians, we should be relational enough to give the maligned party the "benefit of the doubt" while we investigate the negative reports. One idea would be to say to the person bringing the charges: "I'm sorry that you feel that way. That really doesn't sound like my friend. Maybe the three of us should get together to discuss this. When would you like to do it?" At that point, it would be very interesting to hear what the person who is the tale teller replies. This is a "simple but effective" strategy which I learned early on in my days within the military. You would be amazed at how many accusations simply dry up when the accuser is offered the opportunity to meet face-to-face with the one whom they are accusing. I would always give the people who worked for me and with me the benefit of the doubt. I would even give them enough rope to let them hang themselves or skip right on out of trouble if it was a false accusation. It's always important to remember that the one who comes to you with a story or an accusation has a reason for coming to you. Simple but effective truth, and we all know that the Truth will set us free (John 8:32).

Man's Hierarchy

We have focused on apprehending and holding on to the wrong attributes of Father God. We Are Made In His image and likeness and are predestined to become conformed to the likeness of his Son, Jesus Christ through the relational process as we allow Him to refine us. We are not qualified to judge the heart of another and we do not yet see in full God's Plan, for our ways are not yet His ways (Isaiah 55:8). We are not all-knowing and we are not able to discern His final positioning of each and every one of His children. We are, however, called to build up one another in the gifts we have been given, advancing His kingdom through demonstrating His love to one another. *"They will know we are His by our love"* (John 13:35).

We need to stop establishing man's hierarchy and man's requirements for promotion, and instead surrender to Father God's all-knowing heart, trusting Him because: He is good and He is love. We are to trust His Plan and invest our faith that His Will be done on earth as it is in Heaven, for His kingdom always advances. We need to set aside our fear of man and stand firm upon our fear of the Lord! We need to be set apart for His use. Not everything that others attribute to the enemy is truly of the enemy - some of it is actually the Father's Refining Fire; an opportunity given by God for us to be refined as we work through some of the shortcomings of our character, while developing a greater level of Integrity so that we can support the blessing that He has for our lives.

Are we trying to establish a claim to some of the Lord's Glory when we establish man's programs for promotion within the ranks of the Body of Christ? Would it not be humility to surrender our trust to Him and in reverential fear of the Lord simply do our best to train others to seek wisdom through cultivating their own fear of the Lord?

Ministry Time Outs

The Bible tells us that *"what you do to the least of these you do to me"* (Matthew 25:40). What if when we put a new Believer into a time out, we are indicating a lack of trust in the Holy Spirit's ability to train them in using their gifts? What if we're really putting Jesus into a time out?

Calling Others Unteachable

In any instance where we call someone unteachable, we are actually placing a word curse on them. Maybe they just don't respond to our particular style of teaching because they are not wired the same exact way that we are. They may have a completely different Purpose and Destiny in the Lord and will never be a clone of us. Why do we think that to disciple others means that they need to become just like us? Jesus was many different things to each person He encountered and the Lord speaks to each of us differently. The Lord speaks to us in ways that are specifically designed for us to understand because of the way He made us to be. Chances are that if you have 10 different people in a room, you will have 10 totally different and unique definitions of love when you ask each of them to define it. We need to remember that teachers are held accountable to a much higher standard according to the Bible (James 3:1). We need to be careful that we do not practice Charismatic Witchcraft by attempting to control or manipulate those whom we have been entrusted to care for through the discipleship or mentoring process.

Make no mistake - I am not in leadership position within a Church as we tend to consider it. I am actually someone who generally tends to be appreciated more once I have actually moved on from a given place. People often tell me that they did not realize how much they missed me until they run into me again. Perhaps this is because just by nature and personality type, I tend to challenge most people and their definition of friendship. I am an extremely loyal team player and quality acts of service are some of the gifts that the Lord has endowed me with. My early years in the Military developed those gifts as well. When I see something that needs to be done, I tend to simply do it because, after all, we are a team and as soon as these things are done we can focus on the important things. I may not have the gift of Vision, however I do have the gift of Helps which goes hand-in-hand with executing the Vision of those in leadership. Unfortunately, the gift of Helps can often be mistaken for a Spirit of Performance. We need to fine-tune our discernment on this front and not place word curses on a gift set that is of great value to the Body of Christ, especially today as we are trying to bring forth a completely new thing as led by the Lord.

"See, I am doing a new thing" (Isaiah 43:19)… .

If pure Ministry is taking care of widows and orphans (James 1:27), maybe there is a spiritual equivalent whereby those who are particularly challenging people, let's call them Extra Grace Required (EGR or Eager) people may not have a Spiritual Mother or Father. So it is on us to love them into alignment with who they truly are. This could have an extra bonus associated with it because it gives us the opportunity to grow in Grace!

Spiritual Maturity

Time in the Lord does not equal maturity or greater spirituality. Do not allow the world's way of thinking fool you into believing that someone who appears to have a longer or deeper walk with the Lord has no wounds left within their heart. It is our deepest wounds which are most familiar to us and cause us to view the world in a consistently skewed way. Our life's experiences actually color our view of the world and as humans we are predisposed to seeking validation for our view of the world. This means that in any situation where there are several plausible explanations for a given behavior, we tend to pick the explanation which mirrors our own heart's condition best. In other words, if I am a highly motivated by a need for power because of a childhood where I was continuously not in control of the events around me, I will tend to attribute the motivation of control to the actions of others. I would be inclined to desire a position of power and as such, would think that others are also led by that same motivation. Whereas if I am angry about having been treated poorly in life, I will always believe that others act out of anger. The Bible tells us that out of *"the abundance of the heart the mouth speaks"* (Matthew 12:34). In other words, I am transferring the way in which I see the world onto others as their motivation for the way in which they act. The problem is that only God knows the heart of a man (1 Kings 8:39) and I am not qualified to judge the actions of another.

Watchmen on the Wall

There is a trickle down effect as we pour into someone as a Spiritual Mother or Father, whereby we get a blessing as well when there is fruit in their lives. It is important to realize that if we want to receive this blessing, we need to continue to pour blessings into them. We need to continue to be watchmen on the wall always praying for others and we cannot allow ourselves to get distracted by what is going on in our own lives or within the world. We cannot allow ourselves to fall asleep and stop praying unceasingly for one another. We need to continuously lift up our Brothers and Sisters as well as our Sons and Daughters and we need to be active watchmen on the wall in order to do that successfully.

We need to realize that there is an entire generation which feels faceless and nameless; they were brought up in this world by parents who treated them as if they were inconvenient or as if they did not count because they themselves were so wounded or hurt by their own upbringing that they had no love left over to invest into their sons and daughters.

As the Body of Christ, we need to seek the Father's Heart for these ones who tend to be unloveable and we need to speak into their lives, making sure they know just how valuable they are. We need to stick it out in that harvest field, no matter how dirty we get as we seek out these treasures who are still stuck in the world. We need to be willing to dig deep and always be willing to pull out the gold in that nameless, faceless generation because if we don't do it, we will have missed our moment! We will have missed the heart of the Father. We will have missed an opportunity to store up our treasure in heaven, and we will have missed bringing an entire generation into the Kingdom.

We need to make sure we continue to pray unceasingly that we would always see the one in front of us, and that we would see them through the eyes of the Father as well as through the lens of His covenant with us. We need to pray that we would be able to bless those who have not yet been embraced by the rest of society, in Jesus' mighty Name.

Discipling Others to Launch Them into Their Destiny

The days of holding on to people as Spiritual Sons and Daughters are over. The Day of the Harvest of the Lord is upon us and we need to start launching other people into their Destinies. We need to train them to hear from God and we need to equip them to walk out their Salvation (Philippians 2:12) with Him as they in turn introduce others to Jesus. When the Revival that everybody has been speaking and praying into for however many years gets going full swing, it is entirely possible that a thousand people will be added to each Church each week. That is mind-boggling! How exciting to be on the Eve of such an amazing time! However, it's also a time where we need to fulfill our responsibility as Spiritual Mothers and Fathers. We Need to train them up in the Word (Proverbs 22:6), train them up in how to apply His Word as contained in the Holy Bible to their lives, and train them in how to present Jesus to others who have not yet encountered Him (2 Corinthians 5:20). The greatest gift that we could ever give to God is releasing our Spiritual Sons and Daughters into His Kingdom, fully equipped and confident that they hear from Him (John 10:27) as they are led by the Holy Spirit. We need to store up our treasure in Heaven (Matthew 6:19-20), not hold onto it down here on Earth.

Letter to My Leaders,

"Touch Not My Anointed! Stop over-correcting and judging my children. Your job is to edify.
Your job is to grow in grace. Your job is to demonstrate faith. Your job is to trust me. I Am the one who has instructed you to wait until the Harvest to separate the wheat from the tares.
I will send the angels to gather both the wheat and the tares and then separate the wheat from the chaff. Your job is to build up the Body – to encourage everyone to gather together in unity and to grow together in grace."

When Jesus walked with His disciples, He trained them and imparted Kingdom ways to them and then sent them out in authority to do His Father's business. As they returned, they were becoming boastful as they compared stories of the miracles they had done and even went so far as to offer to call down fire upon a city which had not received Jesus well. Jesus simply pointed out that they were beginning to head off the straight and narrow by saying, *"You are of the wrong spirit."* (Luke 9:55) At that point, most of us would have reconsidered the wisdom of continuing to equip and endorse them for ministry, however, Jesus not only continued, He sent out 70 more; He corrected them gently, bringing them back on track, and sent them out once again. There was no forced time out. No punishment. No ending of the program and no closing down of their Ministry. Jesus was focused on training, activating and empowering His Disciples, and He directed us to follow Him! He also instructed us to pray, unceasingly. He never once told us to correct others mercilessly. Remember…as you measure so shall you meet. (Matthew 7:2)

Points to Ponder

Why is it that we always declare that someone is "in Rebellion" as soon as they indicate that they have heard something different from the Lord then what we heard?

Why is it that the very first tendency we have upon hearing someone's new Assignment from the Lord is to introduce doubt and to try to cause them to question whether or not they really heard from the Lord?

Why is it that we seem to believe that we hear from the Lord more clearly on behalf of another then they themselves do? If that's the case, have we done our job to disciple them? Have we trained them and equipped them and lifted them up as we encourage them to cultivate their own ability to hear from the Lord?

Why is it that when someone hears of a new Assignment from the Lord that is going to cause them to no longer do the things that they did for our ministry, picking up the slack and doing things others would not do, and they are no longer going to be available to conveniently be used by us to further our own Ministry, that we suddenly decide that they are in Rebellion?

The Lord wants to be your Sanctuary - press in to Him. Others will be offended by your choices and may even stumble because of their mistaken beliefs just like the Sadducees and Pharisees did in Biblical times, but you will be safe as you pursue the Lord. **He** is your stronghold. Always share the testimony of the Lord and teach those whom you are discipling to listen to and fear His voice first and foremost. We should always bring every new thing that we hear straight back to the Lord, no matter who our source was. We cannot risk blindly following the majority of Believers or even allowing them to discourage us from our path - your path is unique and specific to your Purpose in the Lord. How could another person possibly understand what you are called to do with Him? Let His voice be the one that you follow. Follow Jesus - His people know His voice!

Time for the Bride to Ready Herself

If you are believing these are the LAST days, and are hoping Jesus is coming soon, what sort of a Bride do you feel Jesus deserves? A Bride who has made herself ready? A Bride walking in strength and authority by His side into the dawning of eternity? Or do you think He will return for a Bride who is frozen in fear, just praying to be rescued from the world she found herself in after she woke up from a long slumber?

When Jesus returns, every knee will bow acknowledging Him as KING of Kings and the LORD of Lords (Philippians 2:10-11). Don't you think that He is interested to know who freely CHOOSES to worship Him today while it is still a choice?

The Bible offers us a roadmap for our lives as Christians, and has often been referred to as "Basic Instructions Before Leaving Earth". It instructs us to *"be transformed by the renewing of our minds"* in Romans 12:2 and Jesus continually invites and instructs us to *"Follow Me."* This offers us great hope as it promises that by applying scripture to our lives, we will slowly but surely be changed and as we follow the example of Jesus, we will begin to look more and more like Him! What a glorious promise!!!

The Bible offers us many invitations as well as promises. There are many instances where Jesus through parables provoked the people to reconsider the way they thought about their circumstances. Jesus never wants us to settle for things simply being "the way they are", rather, Jesus invites us to partner with Him for the Kingdom of God, His Father's Will, to be made manifest on earth as it is in Heaven. There are numerous instances where the Bible tells us that no one can know when the Lord will return, not even Jesus. *"But the day of the Lord will come as a thief in the night…therefore what manner of people should you be in holy conduct and godliness, looking for and hastening the coming of the day of God"* (2 Peter 3:10-12a). I believe that this offers us an opportunity to "get in the Game" by choosing to make ourselves ready by being transformed from glory to glory. As we are transformed more and more through the washing of the word and the power of the Blood of Jesus which conquered everything on the cross, we will begin to resemble Him more and more.

As we come alive in Him, we will be better equipped to help disciple others and we shall overcome by the Blood of the Lamb, the Word of our testimony and not loving our old lives unto death! (Revelation 12:11) The Bible also instructs us to pray unceasingly (1 Thessalonians 5:16) and I believe it is time for our fervent prayers to rise to the heavens on behalf of the Bride who needs to rise to the occasion and make herself ready to be His Bride.

I hear the hope of intercession
Raising to the upper heavens,
Calling on God's intervention,
Partnering for His intentions.
As we scale the Seven Mountains
Let our praise ring loud and true-
Right here in the midst of darkness
We place our trust in You!
Lord, You are our all in all.
More than sufficient is your glory!
Just when I had no further to fall,
You raised my head and changed my story.
Thank you, Father, for Heaven's army
Thank you Jesus for your Blood!
It is only by your Spirit
That I move and breathe.
Thank you Lord for restoration.
Thank you for a time such as this!
I never want to miss a moment
In your exquisite presence, for it is Bliss!

Eternal Hope in Christ

He Still Speaks

We should always be cultivating our ear to hear Jesus no matter what our culture tries to tell us. We need to get to that level of Christian commitment where we always look to the Lord to see what He would have us do or say, rather than simply going with the flow of public opinion. The Politically Correct Spirit has neutered today's Church by silencing our voice on key topics of spiritual importance. In short, we as the Church have been more concerned with what man might say than with what the Lord is asking us to stand firm upon. Rather than blending in by simply bemoaning the state of our society, we need to rise up and let our light shine and take a stand for purity and justice. We need to walk in Truth and demonstrate the difference Jesus has made in our lives so that others can see there is hope for them as well. We need to actually testify to the power of Jesus in our lives by including Him in all areas of our lives rather than simply relegating Him to our Sunday mornings. We need to actually allow Him to lead us in our daily lives.

Points to Ponder:

Why is it that within our culture we cherish our ability to be self-sufficient and encourage a Spirit of Independence once we are considered grown up, yet when it comes to our Spiritual development, most of us are willing to settle for what someone else "hears" for us, or for someone else's interpretation of the Word of God, or their idea of

278

what is important for our "takeaway" on a particular Sunday?

When we have a particular area of challenge in our lives, why do we continually seek the input of others, either through prayer or a word, rather than seeking the Lord in greater measure for ourselves and standing firm on His word and promises for our lives?

There comes a time when we are the only one who can walk out His Plan for our lives and we need to be confident that we are able to hear His voice for ourselves. The wisest thing we can do is to cultivate our ability to hear His small, still voice and know that *"His sheep hear His voice."* (John 10:27) When we are faithful with the little things, He will trust us with greater things (Luke 16:10). He wants to know that we trust Him and His voice above the voice and opinions of man. I would prefer to store up my treasure in heaven (Matthew 6:20) and know how to walk forward by faith (2 Corinthians 5:7) rather than depend upon the opinions of others.

While we need to always pray unceasingly (1 Thessalonians 5:16) for one another, and to lift one another up, Father God has a specific Plan for each one of us and a Divine Purpose that is unique to our particular assignment. He wants us to be in relationship with one another and to have accountability with others so that iron can sharpen iron (Proverbs 27:17) as we gain spiritual maturity and move on from being fed milk as infants to actually searching out meat (1 Corinthians 3:1-3) for ourselves as He leads us along the path He has for our specific walk with Him.

Jesus told His disciples that *"I have meat which you know not of"* (John 4:32) when they returned to where He was waiting for them at the Well in Samaria. He was indicating that as He did the Will of the Father and spoke life to the one in front of Him, He was fed spiritually. When we allow the Spirit to flow through us to others, we cannot help being fed spiritually as well! The more time we spend with the Lord in worship and praise, the more we are transformed, and the more we look like Him. What a great promise…that we can truly be transformed from glory to glory (2 Corinthians 3:18) through the renewing of our minds as we learn His thoughts about who we are and who He made us to be…all we need to do is believe in Him and follow Him as He leads us into ever increasing freedom, for where the Spirit of the Lord is, there is freedom (2 Corinthians 3:17)! Hallelujah to the LORD of Lords!

Adventures with The Lord

I love the different ways The Lord speaks to us. One of my favorite things to do is to play "Bible Roulette" to learn what He wants to share with me. I simply ask Him to show me what He wants and then close my eyes and open my Bible. Each time I do this, He will give me several seemingly different scriptures which all completely confirm each other when I ponder them following His direction.

Some people may have a problem with this and try to tell me that it is vital to take and consider the Bible and the Scriptures within their entirety and also within context. This is truth as well. However, when I ask The Lord what He wants to tell me and I then let The Holy Spirit guide me, I am in reality worshipping Him in Spirit and in Truth. **I am NOT trying to establish Doctrine**, rather I am seeking His heart for the moment I am in. I am listening to what He says and not seeking man's wisdom or opinion.

That being said, I would like to share what He shared with me yesterday as I spent time with Him seeking His heart to learn what He wanted me to share at a church in Brasil one night. The first place He opened my Bible to was Joshua Chapter 19 which was a complete confirmation as He had directed both of the other people I was with to the Book of Joshua as well! He highlighted that our *"inheritance was within the inheritance of the children of Judah...for the share of the children of Judah was too much for them."* Jesus is the Lion of the Tribe of Judah and in Him we have been given every Spiritual blessing we could ever need (Ephesians 1:3). These blessings should fill us to overflow, allowing us to minister to others from that overflow.

The Lord then directed me to Isaiah Chapter 50:4-5 and 50:7 reminding me that:

The Lord has given me the tongue of the learned that I should know how to speak a word in season to him who is weary. He awakens me morning by morning. He awakens my ear to hear as the learned. The Lord God has opened my ear. And I was not rebellious. Nor did I turn away, ... for the Lord God will help me therefore I will not be disgraced.

The Lord wants us to know that because of Christ, we have access to solutions for others if we will incline our ear to Heaven to hear His thoughts for them. He has a lot to say to His children if we will only take time to hear His heart for them and then share His heart with others. When we listen to His direction and are obedient, we will not be disgraced!

The Lord then led me to Psalm 96:1-3 where He highlighted the following verses:

Sing a new song to The Lord...Declare His glory to the Nations...His wonders among all peoples.

Our hearts should be overflowing with the Love of The Lord and we should have a new song of worship in our hearts! We should be declaring the glorious things He has done for us to all people and nations for the Book of Revelation tells us that we *"overcome by the Blood of the Lamb, the Word of our testimony, and not loving our lives unto death."* Our very lives should point to His transforming presence within our hearts. As we share our estimony with others, they should catch fire for a life with The Lord as well.

The Direction of the Lord

How many times have you been midstream in a Ministry project only to find your way blocked or you experienced a major course change - like the saying about changing horses in midstream? I don't know about you, but I guess I tend to be a bit like Peter in that whenever I begin to see the possibility that the Lord has for me, I am like:

> "where is my War Horse? I need a horse! Let me get going full tilt... I see the giant just over the horizon and therefore that must be what the Lord wants me to go after... This is the promised land after all... Therefore there must be Giants to be slain... After all, I am more than a conqueror for Christ!"

Anyway, you get it. Not grandiosity, just heavy duty dedication to the one I love, the one who lifted my head and dried my tears and said "Go and sin no more" … The one who truly loved me and saw promise in me despite my depth of confusion about life and Christianity. He saw just who He made me to be and loved me (still does by the way). He encouraged me because He had faith in me, probably far more faith than I ever had in me. I mean, I wanted to be a better version of me, I just had no idea of how to get there! But God! He knew that I could do all things in Christ Jesus - I just had to get into the right position. That position where I was fully in Christ Jesus - not just part way in but all in! There is a process by which we come into alignment with the Lord's Plan for our lives. It's not simply "BAM!" and you are there. It is a process. It is through relationship. The relationship of a lifetime with the Maker of the Universe, Our Father God, His son, Jesus Christ, the one who gave His all that we might have life more abundant, and the Holy Spirit who guides, directs, refines and comforts us as we go through the process of being refined by the Master.

As our relationship with the Trinity grows and our faith develops through His love, we will be inspired to demonstrate our faith and follow Him, walking out His Plan for our lives and testifying to His glory and what He has done for us in order to bring His light and hope and love to others who are still in the depths of darkness and despair. The challenge is, waiting on His best for us. Waiting on His timing. Because the moment that we first see a thing is not usually the moment for us to go after that thing. Sometimes we need to stand firm upon the promises that God has given us, declaring and decreeing them until they are made manifest within our lives. Other times, we're not yet ready to uphold a given promise because we need additional refining in order to be able to not be taken out by the fulfillment of that promise. And then there's always God's timing. Remember, a day is as 10,000. Yes, God's timings are different than ours - He has eternity to work with and "our lives are but a vapor".

Seriously, if God wore a watch what time zone would it be set on? Time as we know it is a man-made constraint. Our calendar actually had to be adjusted and have two additional months added to it because of the inaccuracy of it; the months of July and August were added after the fact. So it is clear that our understanding of time leaves a bit to be desired.

It is important that we do not limit God because He can and will do all things. He just needs for us to cultivate patience as we "wait upon the Lord" and enter into His rest. Trust Him. Allow Him to guide you and refine you. Abandon yourself to the process. God works all things together for the good of those who love Him and are called according to His purposes. Do you trust Him? Are you called according to His purposes, not your man-made purposes, but **His** purposes? Ask Him to confirm what you thought you heard. Ask Him for the next step for you to take. Ask Him to "direct your path". Let His word be a lamp unto your feet. Remember, a bicycle and a car, as well as a boat cannot be steered or directed until they are actually in motion, moving, or being propelled forward. You may ask me what is the similarity between a bicycle, a car and a boat? Well, they are all vehicles which take us from point A to point B. They are also considered to represent ministries. Here's an interesting twist on that theme - just a point to ponder: *what if we really are the hands and feet of Jesus and our ministry is really His ministry and He wants to steer it?!* Maybe we need to let go of our attempts at controlling things and let Him have His way. Because He knows the timing and He knows His perfect Plan. Co-labor means work with Him, within Him, that's where real relationship begins. When we surrender to the obedience of Christ is when we fully come into alignment with Him!

Kingdom Hide and Seek

The Lord is inviting every one of His children to join Him in a game of Kingdom Hide and Seek! For *"it is the glory of God to conceal a matter, but the glory of kings is to search a matter out"* (Proverbs 25:2). Jesus explains the Kingdom of God as a *"treasure hidden in a field which a man found and hid; and for joy over it he goes and sells all that he has and buys that field"* (Matthew 13:44). I believe this refers to us as the treasure and that Father God sent His only Son to pay the price for our redemption, to set us free from where we were stuck, buried in the world, slowly dying.

The Bible also tells us that we *"have this treasure in earthen vessels"* (2 Corinthians4:7). The Lord has placed gifts within each of us and it is to His glory when we choose to partner with Him by seeking out the gifts within another. *"For we are God's fellow workers; you are God's field"* (1 Corinthians 3:9). The Lord is all about relationship; He wants a relationship with each of us directly and He wants us to seek out relationships with our brothers and sisters as well. He invites us to *"seek ye first the kingdom"* (Matthew 6:33), telling us that after we have found that, all the other things we are looking for will fall into place.

I believe that as we choose to partner with Him, seeking out the Kingdom treasure in one another, we will realize that *"indeed the kingdom of God is within"* (Luke 17:21). He wants us to participate, for *"the kingdom of God does not come with observation"* (Luke 17:20). It is time for us to rise to the wonderful opportunity placed before us and begin to shift our focus from the circumstances of this world to looking for the treasure within each person we meet!

"What you do to the least of these, you do unto me." (Matthew 24:40)

The "least of these" would be widows and orphans, both literal and spiritual widows and orphans. Prisoners are also the "least of these" - those in physical prison, as well as those in spiritual prison. Infants in Christ - how we treat them actually reflects how we are considering Christ to be in them. We need to be careful to not quench the spirit that is just developing within them. We need to be careful to not introduce doubt. We need to remember that people live up to how we treat them and they're just beginning to come alive spiritually; this is also true for those who are not yet saved - we need to treat them the way we would our Brothers and Sisters in Christ because, once again, people live up to how we treat them. **The key is do all things as unto the Lord!**

When we question the decisions of another or whether they are truly consulting the Lord before heading out on a given change of direction, we might just be questioning the Lord Himself! Why is it that we seem to think that our idea of what someone else should pursue is us hearing from the Lord more clearly for them than they are hearing from the Lord themselves? The key is: *"no eye has seen, nor ear heard, nor the heart of man imagined what it is that the Lord is preparing for those who love him"* (1 Cor 2:9). We need to realize that **we just do not know everything yet** and we need to give others the benefit of the doubt by realizing that if we have done our part to disciple them truly and built them up in the Lord truly, giving them a strong and proper foundation in Christ, maybe they are hearing the Lord and their walk is just very different from ours!

Luke 12:26 specifically asks: *"if you then are not able to do the least, why are you anxious for the rest?"* This scripture is really sound in pointing us back to the basics - if we're not willing to just begin small and low, pursuing His lead as we cultivate humility, God is by no means going to elevate us. Once again, the wisest thing we can ever choose to do is to always take things back to Father God and ask Him what He wants us to know in each and every situation? We should also be teaching this vital concept to everyone we disciple as well.

Walking on the Water

The Lord is always wanting to stretch us, to expand our tent pegs spiritually. The Bible tells us of how Jesus asked Peter to step out into something new, to get out of his comfort zone, by getting out of the boat he was familiar with in order to walk on water!

"So He said come (Jesus to Peter) and when Peter had come out of the boat, he walked on water
to go to Jesus. But when he saw that the wind was boisterous, he was afraid; and beginning to sink,
he cried out saying 'Lord save me'." (Matthew 14:29)

Jesus asked Peter to do something completely new. Peter stepped out in faith and when he realized how unpredictable the waves and seas were, he leaned on the Lord. What if the seas in this parable of life with Jesus were actually representative of walking in the Spirit by completely trusting in the Lord and His leading? Sometimes the Spirit can be extremely unpredictable, even rough to the point of violence. After all, the Bible even warns us: *"the kingdom of Heaven is led (or advancing) by force, and the violent are seizing it by force."* (Matthew 11:12) This implies an unpredictability as well as a raw power associated with the spiritual realm.

As people, we can tend to become creatures of habit. We want to be able to figure out our world in order to be successful within it. We want to develop a pattern that we are used to so that we know what to expect. When we really step out and follow Jesus, walking in Spirit and in Truth, it can stretch us. It can challenge all we know and have become familiar with, stretching us to fully trust in Him. We need to fully rely upon Him as the uncharted waters of the Spirit will assuredly stretch us.

Throughout His "life" on earth, Jesus showed us the Great Commission and what the possibilities could look like within the Kingdom. However, no one can truly prepare us for what it will actually feel like when we surrender our own free will and step out in faith to truly walk in the spirit…it is experiential, not simply knowledge. When we choose to follow Jesus, He will always point us towards the Tree of Life, giving us an opportunity to step into the pursuit of Life, and Life more Abundant.

Your Time is Always

Jesus said to His brothers: *"my time is not yet come, but your time is always here."* When we have Jesus with us, in our hearts, we should always be ready. We should always be focusing on Him and what He wants to bring forth in each situation rather than allowing circumstances to overwhelm us. Each moment can become a Divine Appointment when we choose to look to heaven to see what the Kingdom possibilities are.

Jesus came across a fig tree and even though it was not the season for figs, He checked it for fruit. When it did not have fruit for Him, He cursed it. The next day the disciples saw it was completely dead. The fig tree should have recognized its Master and produced fruit as Jesus always brings Life and Life more abundant (John 10:10). When we intentionally bring Jesus into every experience, things will shift and the Kingdom will become more and more evident as we step into life more abundant while following Jesus as the Lord of our lives.

Jesus is Always Concerned With the Spiritual

In one instance, Jesus prays for a blind man and then asks what he sees. The man says he sees *"men like trees."* Jesus prays again and the man says his eyes are completely healed (Mark 8:24). I do not believe Jesus actually needed to pray twice. I believe that His first prayer opened the man's Spiritual eyes and he saw the disciples and described them as trees for the Bible says we will become like oaks of righteousness planted by streams of Living water (Jeremiah 17:8) hence, the man saw "men like trees". I believe Jesus then prayed for the man's natural eyes to be opened. Jesus is always most concerned with our Spiritual condition for the Spirit is Eternal while the natural man is merely a vapor (James 4:14), passing away quickly.

We have been given every spiritual blessing in Jesus (Ephesians 1:3)! In the Book of the Revelation of Jesus, it says: *"on each side of the river is a Tree of Life producing twelve kinds of fruit yielding its fruit every month of the year and its leaves are for the healing of the nations."* (Revelation 22:2) We are to be ready in ALL seasons and that which we have been given in Jesus is for the healing of the nations!

I hear the Lord asking:

Would you be willing to be sprinkled out?

Are you willing to have a little bit of you left behind wherever you go that could continuously be used to nourish and enrich those just beginning to develop their Kingdom Roots?

Would you be willing to focus on simply sharing of yourself with the one in front of you and trusting me (the Lord) to put together the bigger picture overall?

Would you submit to the Truth that that which looks to be the least in the world's eyes is that which is most valuable to me?

Will you trust me in the minor details?

Will you let me handle things – orchestrating a master Symphony of your life, note-by-note, while I play you as an instrument bringing the world to its knees by the beautiful simplicity of our walk, hand-in-hand in harmony, with me in the lead and you trusting in me and investing your faith in My Kingdom?

Saturated by grace,
I feel your embrace
Drawing me ever deeper
As I longingly seek your face.
Reigning down from Heaven
You drench us in your love,
Perfecting our broken places.
We are freed to thrive once more,
No longer empty in our searching,
We have been found by the one we adore!
The one who holds us together
No matter what we face!

Eternal Hope in Christ

The Narrow Gate/Denying Jesus

There is a foundational precept which I have noodled on for many years now without becoming convinced that I fully understand it. It's the concept that many are called, but few are chosen. I find myself thinking about this and wondering: well, if many are called why is it that only a few are chosen?

As I Ponder this, one of the things that I cannot help but also consider is the scripture that tells us in Jesus's own words that: *"If you deny me before men, I will deny you before my father."* Jesus goes a step further in explaining Himself in Mark 9:38, by stating: *"For whoever is ashamed of Me and My sayings in this adulterous and sinful generation, of him the Son of Man also will be ashamed when He comes in the glory of His Father with the holy angels."* When I take these scriptures together, I find myself really feeling that I need to always be continuously trying to "up my game" so to speak.

I believe there are many different ways in which we can deny Jesus. Are we denying Him by not taking a Christian stand in difficult conversations? Are we denying Him by not offering to pray with someone when we know that He would step in and heal them when we pray in His Name because we have faith in His Name? Are we denying Him by not fully revealing the depth of our belief and trust and faith in Him to each person we meet? There are many different ways to deny Him and even Peter who had been with Him in person was caught off guard by the fact that he actually denied Jesus three different times and in three different ways before the rooster even crowed. Mark 9:38 actually warns us that if we are even: "uncomfortable/ashamed of Jesus and His sayings", we are in danger of having Jesus be ashamed of us!

As I consider these scriptures, I am continuously made aware of the fact that Jesus presented a standard to the world that was very different from our worldly standards. He stated that if we are even angry at another man we have as good as murdered him ...that's a very different standard then what we consider when we think about the Ten Commandments. The only real conclusion that I come to as I consider these scriptures is that I know for sure that I don't want to be found lacking when I leave the "land of the living" here on earth. I don't want to be one of the 10 foolish virgins who didn't have enough oil to make it through the dark night while waiting for the Bridegroom. I don't want to be left behind.

Over the course of my life there have been many instances where I thought I had most things figured out only to find out that I had missed something pretty major and this is not going to be another one of those times! I'm going to press into Jesus for all I am worth and I am going to go to whatever length I need to in order to let others know that He offers real hope today for our worldly maladies. I'm going to share encouragement with each person I meet and I'm going to offer to pray with each person that the Lord highlights for me to pray with because I don't ever want to deny Him the chance of touching someone who He paid the price for over 2000 years ago (and He paid the price for every person who chooses to receive Him as Lord and Savior). In short, I don't want to fall short of His Kingdom standard. I want my name to be known in heaven and I want to recognize His precious face in my own as I grow closer to Him each and every day.

The Spirit of Entitlement and The Politically Correct Spirit

Through poor choices, man has cut himself off from the Lord, as well as from each other. Division and strife have led to Racial divide which was never part of God's Plan. We are at the pinnacle moment and our next choices have the potential to drastically affect us - do we choose love or do we choose Entitlement and a false sense of security, wrapped tightly in our Differences as we jump up and down trying to out shout one another about how valuable we are and what our particular "Title" is? We need to lay it all down at the foot of the Cross. We need to choose the lower road and prefer others before ourselves. We need to bare our hearts to Jesus that if there is any sense of Entitlement or any Racial Prejudice hidden within our hearts, Jesus would remove it. We need to lift up His mighty Name and we need to ask to be healed from our tendency to seek out Division rather than Unity. We need to continuously choose Love. We need to empower one another as we learn how to hear Jesus more and more clearly as we follow Him. We need to fervently pray that each one of us gets rightly aligned with God and steps right into the middle of our own unique Divine Purpose so that the Body of Christ can walk forward together in Unity, setting aside our differences once and for all!

What if the direction to "pick up your Cross" was never meant to be a burden for us, but rather an invitation to go back to the Cross where Jesus first demonstrated His Love for us, to pick up that Love and wrap it around us and then head out so that the world would know we are Christians by our Love? What if satan got a hold of that idea and twisted it and got us off track and now look where we are - thinking that it's a burden to demonstrate Love to anyone who is not exactly like us? What if he then further twisted our concept of Love and made it to where we think that in order to love someone, we have to show that we approve of them and that's what ushered in a lot of his agenda through the "Politically Correct" Spirit? What then?

In Closing

My main purpose in writing this is to give hope to those who are struggling and to share some of the strategies that the Lord gave me for overcoming some challenging moments in my life. The only way we will overcome is by choosing to receive the power of the Blood of Jesus within our lives and then sharing our testimony of what He has made possible for us in order that another brother or sister in Christ can be set free. The testimony of what Jesus has done for us is the Spirit of Prophecy because what He has done for one He wants to do for others. Are we willing to step into our new lives as overcomers and share our testimony so others may also receive their breakthrough? Are we willing to recalibrate our compasses to True North by applying the Bible to our lives today? Are we willing to stand firm on His promises and offer hope to a dark world by letting our lights shine brightly in a world which espouses freedom of speech but silences any talk of Jesus? The Master we serve while on earth will be the one we spend eternity with and there is no tolerance for being a lukewarm Christian in the Kingdom. There is no more time to mull over the vast choices of all the counterfeit gods satan has created for worship within the world; if you are not choosing Jesus you are denying Him. Period. Satan has done his homework and he knows the time is short. He knows that if he can just get a couple of twists into our understanding of the scriptures, the longer we operate based upon lies, the farther away from Kingdom Truth we will be. Satan knows that if he can keep our attention off of Jesus and keep us focused on what he has brought to ruin in our lives, in short our crazy circumstances, he is actually fooling us into worshipping him and what he has done to us. In reality, when we choose to worship something we are choosing to focus our attention upon it. If we are preoccupied with the destruction of our past or the circumstances of the world which overwhelm us, we are focusing on satan and his plan for our destruction. We need to worship Jesus and look to Him knowing that we shall know the Truth and the Truth shall set us free! We are not our circumstances - we never were. That is why it is vital for us to read our Bibles and to sit with the Lord to learn what He says about us and who we are in Christ. The Lord is the only one who knows our complete Destiny and who He made us to be. Our Journey with Him is the beginning of our eternal relationship - won't you choose to pursue a whole new level of intimacy with Him today?

A Final Point to Ponder

The first miracle attributed to Jesus was at the Wedding at Cana where they had run out of wine and His mother, Mary, told Him about it (John 2). Jesus told her that it wasn't His time yet, and Mary simply told the servants to do whatever Jesus told them to do. Jesus then told the servants to fill the six stone water pots to the brim with water and to then pour out some of it to take to the master of the feast. When the master of the feast tasted "the water that was made wine," he was amazed by the quality of it. Notice that Jesus never touched the water or spoke to it, He only told the servants at the wedding to use the six stone water purification pots by filling them to the brim. Throughout the Bible, Jesus tells us that He only ever does what He sees the Father do. I believe that when Mary first spoke to Him, He saw it was not time for Him to do anything, but when Mary exercised extreme faith by telling the servants "whatever He says to you, do it," the very heart of God was moved and the first miracle occurred at Cana. Six is the number which points to man in the Bible and we as men are called to be "living stones" with which He can build His Spiritual house (1 Peter 2:5).

What if Jesus wants to fill us full of His Living Water and use us as living stone vessels to turn that water into the new wine that He can pour out as He invites others in to His Kingdom wedding feast?

Jesus, The Firstfruits

Like some unforgotten treasure
Buried way down deep,
I see you in my dreams-
I hunt you in my sleep.
Your gaze is truly piercing!

Deep calls out to deep

I cannot get my fill
Of the goodness of your presence.
You simply make me weep.
I want you more and more-
My heart burns with your fire
All consuming, oh so sweet.
I give you every thought
And ask to be made anew.
I love you more and more,
A passion I never knew
Although I searched in many places
For a love just like you.
I praise you for your grace
That has made me feel brand new.
You rework my heart
So I resemble you,
More and more,
Simply loving every one brought to me by you.

Eternal Hope in Christ
22 July 2017, Malawi Africa

301

Light Provoked the Darkness

Flashes in the frequency of JOY-
Your Love captivates me-
Steadily healing my heart.

I have plunged in to the deep end of the ocean;
Drawn ever closer by your Word.

You are the one who pieced me back together:
Mending my shattered heart.
Giving me new life.
Teaching me to dance, no matter the circumstance.
You are the one who fills me full-
Bringing warmth to my very core
While igniting my heart.

You have called me to bring
your light to the darkness,
Releasing your Joy
To the restless, those still searching,
Trying to fill the Black Holes of their lives.

You alone are faithful and true

And what you did for me
I know you are longing again to do.
Setting another and another and another

FREE

To walk with you
Straight in to Eternity!

Eternal Hope in Christ

Dancing Down the Aisle with Jesus

Some of our budding dreams
Were plucked by the world
Before they burst forth in bloom.
Some of our deepest desires
Were dashed from our eyes
As tears of disappointment,
Gifts from a cruel world.
But God is weaving them
Into the Bridal veil
We shall wear as we dance
Into eternity on the arm
Of our Loving Groom,
Jesus,
The one who poured
His very heart out
To walk us down the aisle.

Eternal Hope in Christ

References

References are taken from the Bible (NKJV, ESV)

Cover Design by Edith Houghton and Trina Olson

Edith Houghton has been traveling with Radical Launch International Ministries as an Itinerant Minister for the past two years, both within the United States and overseas. She is the Co-founder of Unleashed Publishing, Inc. with Trina Olson along with other Kingdom building projects including a Ministry House in Bull Shoals, Arkansas designed to train and equip others to step into their divine purpose and destiny. Together with Trina, she is currently working to bring forth the JP-5 Project to provide a place for Christians to celebrate the Lord as they are equipped and empowered to walk in the supernatural ways of the Lord while bridging the gap between the secular world and the Kingdom of God.

Edith gave her heart to Jesus at an early age only to then find herself caught up in the world. She served as an Officer in the US Navy where she quickly learned the value of teamwork and the importance of living a life of integrity. Upon rededicating her life to the Lord and giving Him Lordship over her life, Edith's heart was ignited with a passion for the things of God and she attended many of the training opportunities and equipping Conferences at the Global School of Supernatural Ministry (GSSM) under Randy Clark She ministered within the Eastern District in the Baltimore area while going on Ridealongs with the Baltimore Police Department and saw the crime rate reduced to a thirty year low as the Faith-based Initiative was implemented there. Edith enjoys "Power Evangelism" and re-presenting the Love of Jesus to the lost within the inner cities of the United States and abroad as she travels to the nations following the command of Jesus to disciple nations. She is excited to seek out the gold within others and she does her best to encourage and edify the Body of Christ wherever she goes

Unleashed Publishing, Inc.

Unleashing the potential authors,
editors, and illustrators of a
generation.

CPSIA information can be obtained
at www.ICGtesting.com
Printed in the USA
FSHW011308050120
65606FS